An Introduction to
Backgammon

An Introduction to
Backgammon
A Step-by-Step Guide

PAUL MAGRIEL

Times
BOOKS

Acknowledgments

I gratefully acknowledge the advice and help
given me by many friends in preparing this work
for publication. My deepest thanks go to Renee
Magriel, who worked with me at every stage.

An Introduction to Backgammon: A Step-by-Step Guide is an abridged version —
designed for beginning players — of the more comprehensive text, *Backgammon*
by Paul Magriel, Quadrangle/The New York Times Book Co., New York, N.Y.,
1976.

Excerpts from Chapter 1 previously appeared in *The Game of Backgammon* by
Paul Magriel and Penny Mintz. Copyright © 1973 by Topalco Limited, Hong
Kong, B.C.C., and reprinted with their permission.

Library of Congress Cataloging in Publication Data

Magriel, Paul.
    An abridged version of the author's Backgammon.
    I. Backgammon.   I. Title.
GV1469.B2M342   1977   795'.1   77-7727
ISBN 0-8129-0735-3

Contents

Introduction

THE GAME OF BACKGAMMON is easy and fun to learn. It is an ancient and fascinating game that you will be able to play after only a little instruction. The best way to begin is to play along with the book. Make the moves in each game yourself as soon as you can. Don't worry about memorizing every idea or definition at the first reading — come back later to anything that puzzles you. Remember that the key to learning the game is practice, and as you become more familiar with the game, you will have ample opportunity to appreciate the richness and subtlety of the strategy.

If you are a new player, begin with Chapter 1 (Rules). Read quickly through this chapter and Chapter 2 (Notation) to Chapter 3 (Basic Checker Play). When these three chapters are understood, you may begin immediately to play along with the four backgammon games that follow. Each of these games illustrates a different game plan and is followed by a summary of the basic ideas which have been presented. These summaries contain much valuable information that should be studied carefully.

As you practice, begin to incorporate the strategies you have learned into your own play. Study each position in the sample games and figure out your own move first before reading the correct move and explanation in the text. Don't worry if your move is right or wrong — it is important only to practice making your own moves. New terms are introduced and defined throughout the text. If you are unfamiliar with a term, check the Glossary.

Chapters 11 and 12 deal with more technical aspects of the game. Don't be intimidated by these chapters. Remember: backgammon is *not* a game of mathematical calculations. It is primarily a game of position and strategy where you recognize and anticipate visual patterns. Any player can study and easily understand the sample games without spending too much time on the last two chapters.

No matter what your level, I am certain that you will find backgammon extremely enjoyable — both to learn and to play.

P. M.
(X-22)

CHAPTER 1.
RULES

Object of the Game

Backgammon is a dice-and-board game for two players. Each player begins the game with fifteen checkers of a different color from his opponent, a pair of dice, a dice cup, and a doubling cube. Players move their checkers around the board according to the roll of the dice. The first player to get all of his checkers, or men, around and finally off the board is the winner.

In this book, you will be referred to as "X" and your opponent as "O."

Position 1
Starting Position

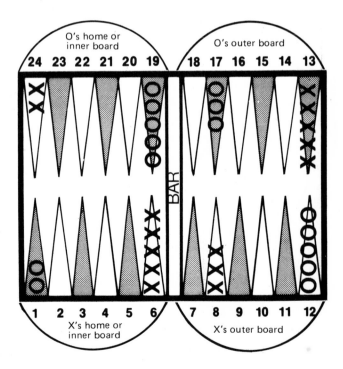

The Board

As Positions 1 and 2 indicate, the playing board has twenty-four triangles called **points,** divided into four quadrants. Each quadrant contains six points. The quadrants are referred to as your (X's) **home** or **inner board,** your (X's) **outer board**, your opponent's (O's) **home** or **inner board,** and your opponent's (O's) **outer board.** The home and outer boards are separated by the **bar.**

Starting the Game

The checkers are initially placed as shown in Position 1. (Alternately, the mirror image of this starting position can also be used, as shown in Position 2.) In this book the starting position for each game will always be Position 1. A new player, however, should be familiar with both positions.

Play begins with each player rolling one die. The player having the higher number moves first. For his first move, he *must* use the two numbers already cast by him and his opponent. Ties are re-rolled but may affect the scoring (see **automatic doubles** at the end of this chapter). After the first throw, each player uses two dice on each turn. Players alternate after each throw.

Position 2
Mirror Image of
Starting Position

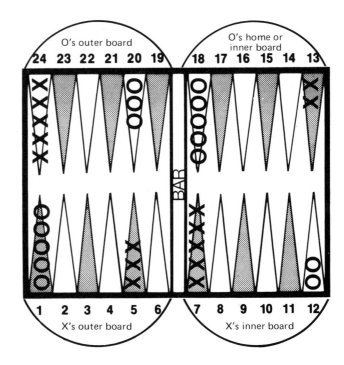

Moving the Checkers

Position 3
Movement of X's
Checkers

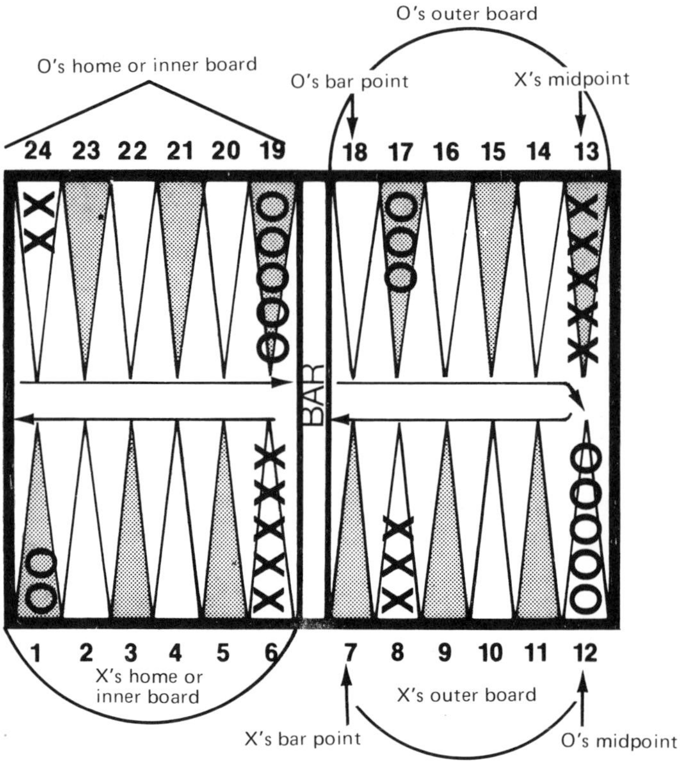

Position 4
Movement of O's
Checkers

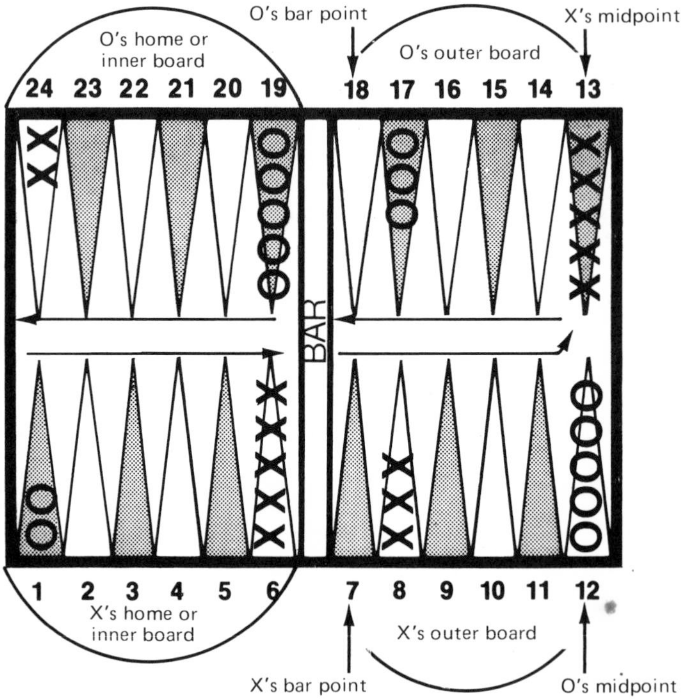

Imagine the board as a U-shaped playing track. Any checker at any point on the board can be advanced around the U, but only by moving it "forward."

The movement of X's checkers is shown in Position 3. For X, "forward" is the line of movement from the twenty-four point to the one point. In other words, X moves from O's home board, over the bar to O's outer board, around the closed end of the U into X's outer board, and finally back over the bar into X's home board. The bar does not count as a point.

The movement of O's checkers is shown in Position 4. Your opponent moves his checkers around the same U-shaped track, *but in exactly the opposite direction as you*. In other words, O moves his checkers from the one point to the twenty-four point. No checker can ever move backward.

The throw of the dice determines the number of **points** or **pips** that checkers may be advanced. The two numbers thrown are considered as two separate moves (though both moves may be made by the same checker) rather than a total. Thus, a throw of 3–5 does not represent one move of 8, but rather two moves: one of 3 and one of 5. A player who rolls 3–5 may advance one checker 3 pips and then advance that same checker another 5 pips (he may play the 5 first and the 3 second); or he may move one checker 3 pips and a different checker 5 pips.

As an example, let us return to the opening position. If X rolls 3–5, three possible moves from the starting position are:

1. X advances a checker 3 pips from the twenty-four point to the twenty-one point, and then advances the same checker 5 pips from the twenty-one point to the sixteen point (as shown in Position 5).

Position 5

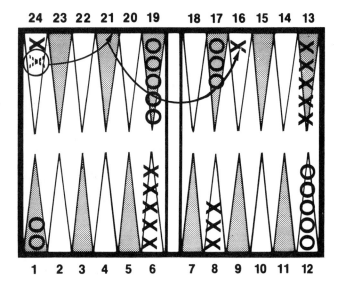

2. X moves one checker down from the thirteen point to the ten point, and moves a second checker down from the thirteen point to the eight point (Position 6).

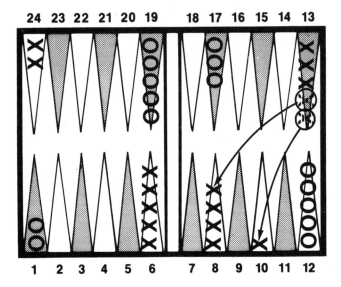

Position 6

3. X moves one checker from the eight point to the three point, and moves another checker from the six point to the three point (Position 7).

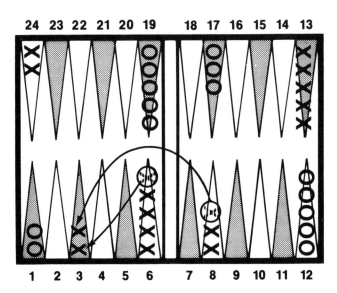

Position 7

Throwing Doubles

Whenever doubles (1–1, 2–2, 3–3, 4–4, 5–5, 6–6) are thrown, a player moves *twice* the number shown on the face of the dice. A throw of 5–5, for example, means that the player has four 5's to move. These moves may be made in any of the following combinations:

1. Move one checker four 5's.
2. Move one checker three 5's and another checker one 5.
3. Move two checkers two 5's each.
4. Move one checker two 5's and two other checkers one 5 each.
5. Move four checkers one 5 each.

Where Checkers May Land

A checker may land on any vacant point. It may also land on any point occupied by a player's own checkers (there is no limit to the number of any one player's checkers that may occupy a single point); or on any point occupied by only *one* of his opponent's checkers. All the points on which a checker may land are called **open points.**

A checker may *not* land on a point that is occupied by *two or more* opposing checkers. You may not even stop at such a point "in passing" when moving a single checker (remember that the two numbers on the dice are considered separate moves). You can, however, pass over points occupied by your opponent.

For example, if X rolls 3–5 when the nineteen and twenty-one points are each occupied by two or more of O's checkers, X cannot move either of his back checkers from the twenty-four point, even though the sixteen point is empty (Position 8).

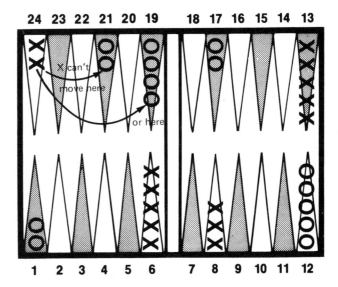

Position 8

If, in Position 8, X were to roll 6–3, he could play his 6 first and then his 3, passing over the blocked twenty-one and nineteen points to land on the empty fifteen point.

A player is not permitted to pass his turn. Both numbers on the dice must be played, if legally possible. Since the entire roll is considered an entity, it is *not* legal to play one number in such a way as to make the other number impossible to play. If only one number can be played, then the *higher* number must be played, if possible. Numbers that cannot be played are forfeited.

Hitting and Re-entering

Two or more checkers of the same color on a point are said to **own** that point. A lone checker is called a **blot.** Should a player's checker land on an opponent's blot, that blot has then been **hit** and is placed **on the bar,** where it is temporarily out of play. (Note that players are not obliged to hit a blot every time they are presented with an opportunity to do so.)

If a player has one or more checkers on the bar, he cannot move any other checker until *all* of his checkers on the bar have been re-entered. A checker on the bar must re-enter the game in the opposing player's home board. This can be done only when the player rolls a number corresponding to an **open point** in his opponent's home board.

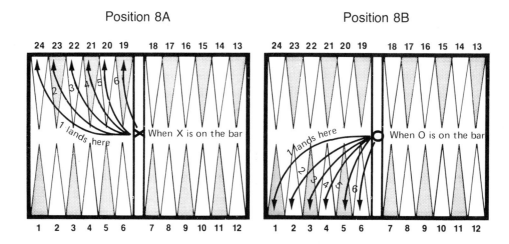

Position 8A   Position 8B

If X rolls a 1 on either die, he may land on the first point (the twenty-four point) in O's home board *if* that point does not contain two or more of O's checkers.

Similarly, if X rolls a 2 he may land on the twenty-three point; a 3, the twenty-two point; 4, twenty-one point; 5, twenty point; 6, nineteen point.

If O has a checker on the bar, a 1 on a die corresponds to the one point in X's inner board. Similarly, if O rolls a 2 he can land on the two point; 3, three point; 4, four point; 5, five point; 6, six point.

The specific number needed to re-enter must come up on at least one die. The *sum* of the two dice is not used to re-enter.

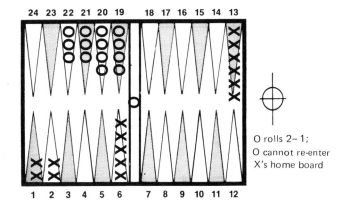

24 23 22 21 20 19   18 17 16 15 14 13

Position 8C
O Rolls 2–1

O rolls 2– 1;
O cannot re-enter
X's home board

For example, in Position 8C the one, two, and six points are owned by X. O is on the bar. If O rolls 2–1 he *cannot* land on the open three point; he must roll a specific 3 on one die to land on that point.

Points occupied by two or more opposing checkers are called **closed points,** and the opponent's checkers cannot land on them. If both numbers on a player's dice correspond to closed points, the player cannot re-enter his checker on that roll. He must wait and try again on his next turn. In the meantime, since he cannot move any of his other checkers either, his opponent continues to move.

In Position 9, O has closed the nineteen, twenty, and twenty-three points. X has one checker on the bar. If X rolls 5–3, he must, before doing anything else, use the 3 to bring his checker on the bar back into play in his opponent's home board. The 5 cannot be used to re-enter because the fifth point in O's inner board, the twenty point, is closed. X must re-enter on the twenty-two point, the third point in O's inner board. After X has re-entered his checker, he may play any legal 5.

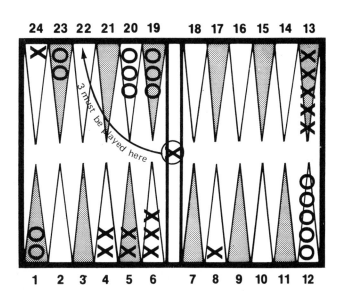

Position 9
X Rolls 5–3

If X rolls 5–2 in Position 9, he would have to give up his turn. Neither the 5 nor the 2 re-enter because both the fifth point (the twenty point) and the second point (the twenty-three point) are closed in O's inner board. The checker on the bar cannot move directly to the eighteen point because the sum of the dice may not be used.

Position 10

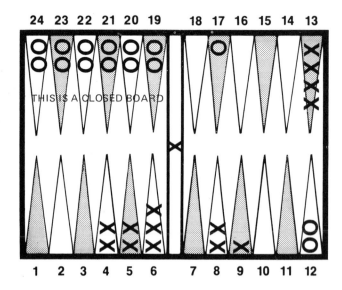

O has all of his home-board points closed and X has a checker on the bar in Position 10. X must wait until one of O's home-board points is opened before he can re-enter his checker from the bar and then continue moving his other checkers.

When you or your opponent closes all six home-board points, this is known as a **closed board.** In Position 10, O would continue to roll until he opened one of his home-board points. Then it would be X's turn to roll.

Bearing Off

Once you have brought *all* your checkers into your home-board, you can begin to remove them. This is called **bearing off.** A checker that has been borne off the board is not re-entered for the rest of the game. If a checker is hit by your opponent during the bearing-off process, no more checkers can be borne off until that checker has re-entered your opponent's inner board and has been brought back to your inner board. The first player to bear off all of his checkers wins the game.

Procedure in Bearing Off: In bearing off, you are, in effect, bringing your checkers just past the first point in your home board.

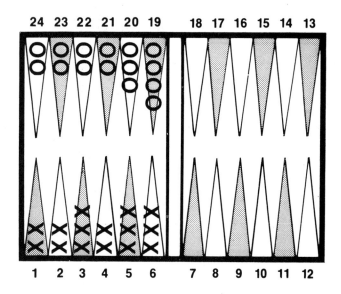

Position 11
X Rolls 6–4

If X rolls 6–4 in Position 11, where he has two or more checkers covering each point in his home board, the 6 must be used to bear one checker off the board from the six point. The 4 may be used to bear off a checker from the four point (as seen in Position 11A).

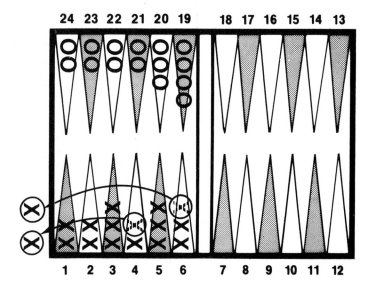

Position 11A

The 4 in 6–4 may also be used to advance a checker from the six point to the two point (Position 11B),

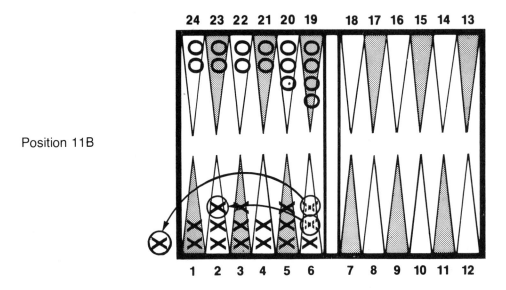

Position 11B

or to advance a checker from the five point to the one point (Position 11C).

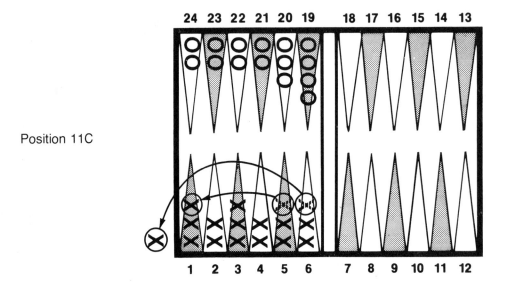

Position 11C

A 2–1 could be used to bear two checkers off: one from the one point and one from the two point; or to bear one checker off the three point by first moving it to the one or two point and then using the remaining number to bear it off.

If a player rolls a number higher than any point on which a checker rests, the checker on the next highest point is taken off instead.

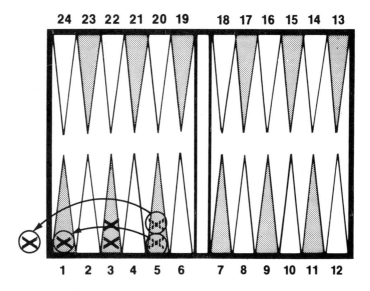

Position 12

In Position 12, X has two checkers on the five point and two checkers on the three point. If he rolls 6–4, the 6 must be played by bearing off one checker from the five point. X cannot now use the 4 to bear a checker off the three point because he still has a checker on the five point and the *full* number must be used whenever possible. Therefore, the 4 *must* be used to move a checker from the five point to the one point.

Similarly, when O is bearing off checkers, a 6 on the dice can be used to bear a man off the nineteen point; a 5 off the twenty point; a 4 off the twenty-one point; a 3 off the twenty-two point; a 2 off the twenty-three point; a 1 off the twenty-four point.

Scoring

The game begins with a value of one point, or unit. This is won by the first player to bear off all his checkers. The **doubling cube,** with the numbers 2, 4, 8, 16, 32, and 64 on its faces, is used for keeping track of the increase in units or points, for which the game is being played.

At the beginning of the game, the doubling cube is placed halfway between the two players with 64 facing up. This indicates that the game is being played for one point. If one player feels he has gained an advantage in the course of play, he may **double** the stakes by turning the cube to 2 and offering it to his opponent. This is done *before* he rolls the dice for his turn. Note that when a player is closed out, he does *not* forfeit his right to double.

His opponent then has a choice: He can refuse the double (or **pass**), thus conceding the game and losing one point; or he can accept the double (**take**), take possession of the doubling cube, and continue playing the game for two points. A player who accepts a double **owns the cube** and is then the only person in a position to re-double the stakes.

The game can be doubled and re-doubled any number of times subject to the following conditions:

1. Initially, the cube is in the middle and either player may double. Subsequently, only the player who owns the cube may re-double. The same player cannot double twice consecutively.

2. A player can only double *prior* to his roll. If the double is accepted by his opponent, the player then proceeds to roll the dice and take his move.

Gammons, Backgammons, and Variations

The player who wins the game scores the number of points indicated on the doubling cube, unless there is a **gammon** or **backgammon.** A **gammon** (or double game) occurs when the winner bears off all of his checkers before his opponent bears off *any* checkers at all. In this case, the winner receives *double* the amount shown on the doubling cube.

A **backgammon** occurs when the winner bears off all his checkers before his opponent bears off any, *and* while his opponent has one or more checkers in the winner's home board. In this event, the winner receives *triple* the points shown on the doubling cube. (Outside the United States, a backgammon is only scored as a double game.)

Here are two variations that players may adopt by agreement *prior* to beginning play:

1. **Automatic Doubles:** If each player rolls the same number on the first roll of the game, the doubling cube remains in the middle, but is turned to 2. Players usually agree to limit the number of automatic doubles to one per game. The players then throw the dice again to see who goes first.

2. **The Jacoby Rule:** If neither player has doubled during the course of a game, gammons and backgammons do not count. They are scored as single games.

Chouette

Chouettes provide an opportunity for three or more people to play in the same backgammon game. To begin a chouette, each person rolls one die. The individual with the highest number becomes the **man in the box** and plays against the remaining people, who act as a team.

The second-highest roller becomes the team **captain.** He actually moves the checkers against the man in the box while his teammates advise. Should disagreements arise among the team players, the captain's decisions are final. The first throw of the dice also establishes the order in which each team member assumes the position of captain in subsequent games.

If the team loses the first game, the captain is replaced by the next player, and becomes last in the team's order of rotation. The man in the box remains in the box. If the team wins, the captain becomes the man in the box, the next team member assumes the captain's position, and the former man in the box becomes the last in the team's order.

The team acts in concert when doubling the player in the box. Should the box double, however, *each* individual team member has the option of accepting or declining. Those declining each lose to the player in the box and drop out of that particular game.

Those accepting the double continue to play as a team for the increased number of points. If they win, they each gain the number of points indicated on the doubling cube from the player in the box. If they lose, they each give up the number on the cube to the man in the box.

Procedure and Courtesy of Play

1. A player must roll his dice in the board to his *right*.

2. A roll is invalid and must be re-rolled if a die lands out of the right-hand board, if it lands cocked, or if it lands on a checker.

3. A player's move is not final until he has picked up his dice.

4. A player may not roll his dice until his opponent has completed his move and picked up his dice. This rule, however, is not strictly adhered to in bear-off situations where no further contact is possible, or when a player's move is forced.

5. Illegal moves may be corrected by either player, but the correction must be made *before* the next player rolls. Any errors not corrected in time remain as played.

CHAPTER 2.
NOTATION

IN·THE DIAGRAMS and text to follow we have developed a simple numerical notation to indicate the numbers rolled on the dice and the movement of the checkers.

Dice Rolls

Numbers rolled on the dice are separated by a dash (–).

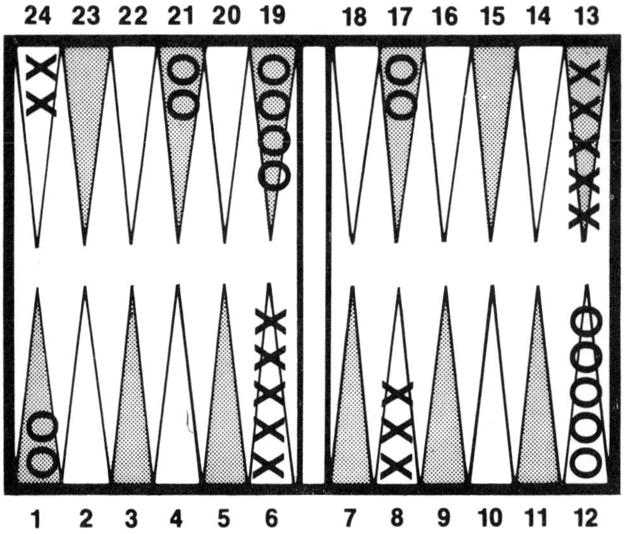

Position 1
X to Play 3–3

In Position 1, the notation X to Play 3–3 indicates that X has double 3's to play.

Occasionally, in demonstrating a particular position, only half a roll (one number on the dice) may be indicated: X to Play 3.

Checker Moves

Typically, as in Position 1, a diagram shows the position *before* the indicated dice roll has been played, in order to enable you to guess beforehand what the move might be.

In many positions — and particularly during the course of describing a game — we also indicate how a man has already moved. Thus when the move (in parentheses) is indicated on the diagram, it has already occurred. The numbers showing a move are separated by a slash (/). The first number indicates the starting point; the second, the landing point. 4/2, for example, indicates that one checker was taken from the four point and moved to the two point.

Position 2
(X 3–3 6/3[2], 8/5[2])

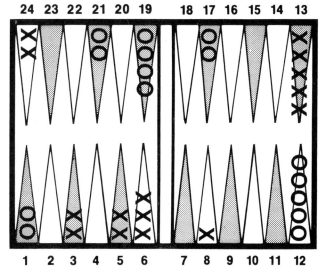

In Position 2, X has rolled 3–3. He has played four 3's. The notation indicates that he moved two men from the six point to the three point 6/3(2) and two men from the eight point to the five point 8/5(2).

When a move, or part of a move, cannot be played legally, the symbol ø is used. 6/1, ø indicates that the player moved one checker from the six point to the one point, but was unable to use the remaining number on the dice. X ø indicates that X was unable to play any part of his roll legally.

Numbering the Points

In this book, points are described (counted) from *X's point of view*. They are numbered one through twenty-four beginning in X's inner board to X's outer board, to O's outer board, to O's inner board.

From O's point of view, however, X's twenty point is the same as O's five point. Occasionally we refer to O's making *his* four point; on the diagram this will appear as the twenty-one point. Also, in general discussions of the value of certain points, we may refer, for example, to a player's five point without further specification. For X, this would refer to the point labeled "five"; for O, the point labeled "twenty."

Hitting

When an opposing checker has been hit, the indicated move is followed by an asterisk (*). In Position 2, let's assume that O rolls 6–1. He plays it by moving one man off the one point to the seven point and then continuing it to the eight point, hitting a blot. The resulting position is shown in Position 3. The move taken is indicated by (1/8*). To repeat, when a move is indicated on a diagram in parentheses, *it has already occurred.*

Position 3
(O 6–1 1/8*)

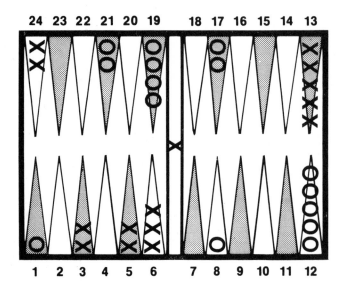

Re-entering from the Bar

When a checker re-enters the game from the bar, the move is indicated by the word *bar* followed by a slash (/), followed by the number of the point the checker landed on. (Bar/22) indicates that a checker from the bar re-entered the game and moved to the twenty-two point.

Bearing Off

When a checker is borne off the board in the latter stages of the game, the move is indicated by the number of the point the checker was moved from, followed by a slash (/), followed by the word "off." 6/off means that a checker on the six point was borne off the board. Checkers already borne off the board are indicated by the X's and O's to the left of the playing surface.

The Cube

The position of the doubling cube in a diagram indicates which player may double next. If neither player has doubled, the cube is in the middle. When the cube is owned by O, it is at the top right of the diagram; when owned by X, at bottom right.

When the cube is not pertinent to a particular position, it is not shown.

Bar Point, Midpoint

Bar always refers to the raised area between the inner and outer boards where a checker rests after being hit.

Bar point refers to the seven point of the player moving the checkers (the eighteen point for O, the seven point for X).

Midpoint refers to the thirteen point of the player moving the checkers (the twelve point for O, the thirteen point for X).

CHAPTER 3.
BASIC CHECKER PLAY

IF YOU HAVE never played a single game of backgammon, the hardest aspect involved initially may be counting pips, or figuring out exactly where a checker goes on a particular move. Although this is a cumbersome task at first, you should carefully count out one point at a time until you become more accustomed to moving the checkers. Don't worry if your first few games seem to be moving slowly — even the best players in the world began by counting one by one.

You will probably discover within a relatively short time that you are moving the checkers more rapidly. When you become less concerned with the mechanics of counting, you will be better able to appreciate the strategy of the game. In any case, the best way to learn backgammon is to play it. Even if you are not always making the theoretically correct play, you will be acquiring valuable experience which will improve your judgment and help you get the feel of the game.

To help the novice player, we begin by giving some exercises in hitting and making closed points. The next chapter illustrates the first sample game. Let us emphasize again the importance of getting out a board yourself, setting up the indicated positions, and making the moves.

Position 1
X on Roll. What Does X
Need to Hit?

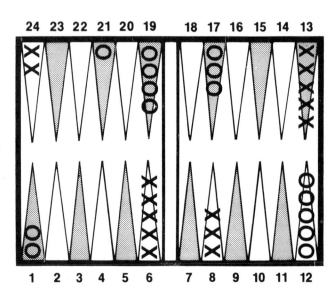

Hitting

X is on roll in Position 1. O has a blot on the twenty-one point. What number does X need to hit this man and send him to the bar?

X needs a 3 to hit. If the number on either die comes up 3, or if the sum of the numbers on the dice enables X to move exactly 3 pips forward, then X may land on the twenty-one point and hit O. In this position, 6–3, 5–3, 4–3, 3–3, 2–3, and 1–3 all hit, as well as 2–1 and 1–1 (because of the doubles rule: X has four 1's to play). A 4 does not hit the blot; it merely passes over it.

In this position, the opportunity which X has to hit O is called a **direct shot.** We define a direct shot as a blot which is 6 pips or less away from an opposing checker. The number needed to hit the blot can show on *either* die, or as a combination of both dice.

When the number needed to hit a blot is 7 or more pips away, we call that a **combination** or **indirect shot.** In that case only a specific combination requiring *both* dice can give the needed number.

A direct shot is much more likely to be hit than an indirect shot. (For specific odds, see Chapter 11.)

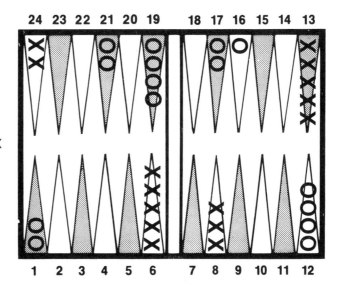

Position 2
X on Roll. What Does X
Need to Hit?

In Position 2, O's blot is 8 pips in front of X's man on the twenty-four point. X therefore needs an 8 to hit. This is an indirect shot. Only a combination of both dice can produce the needed number: 6–2 and 4–4. 5–3 does not hit in this instance because neither the 5 nor the 3 may be played legally from the twenty-four point. Because of the special nature of doubles, 2–2 also hits.

X's men on the thirteen point do not threaten to hit because they cannot move backward.

Note that you do *not* have to hit whenever you have the opportunity to do so; if you do not wish to hit, you may take your move elsewhere.

With more experience in counting, you will know just by looking at the board what numbers hit your opponent and what numbers you yourself are exposed to should you leave a blot. Two hints a new player may find useful in the mechanics of counting are:

1. A man to be moved an *even* total remains on the *same color* point. A man to be moved an *odd* total will *switch colors*. This observation of the color of points facilitates counting and acts as a quick check.

2. Notice that each quadrant is six points long. If you move from one quadrant to the corresponding point in the next quadrant, the move will always be exactly 6 pips away.

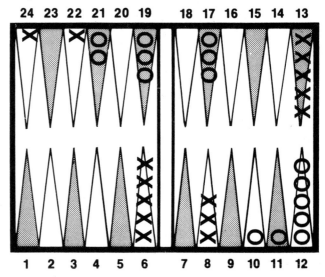

Position 3
X on Roll. What Does X
Need to Hit?

O has two blots in Position 3. Since they are both less than 6 pips in front of X's men on the thirteen point, they are both directly exposed. This is called a **double direct shot** (or **double shot**). Any simple 2 or 3 will hit. A 2–1 hits *both* men, which is particularly dangerous for O. (This would be called a double hit.) 1–1 does not hit because the twelve point is owned by O.

The two blots are also 11 and 12 pips away from X's man on the twenty-two point. 6–5 and 6–6 hit from the twenty-two point, as well as 4–4 (moving three of the four 4's). This shot alone would be a **double indirect shot.**

Remember to keep both your and your opponent's direction in mind!

In Position 4, the blot on the one point is exposed to 5's (a direct shot), and also to 7's and 12's (combination shots). Position 4 is our first example of a case where hitting may be possible but not desirable. To see why, let's briefly examine the reasons for hitting.

As a rule, you try to hit your opponent when possible. By hitting a blot you send it to the bar from which it must re-enter in your inner board — the very beginning of its journey around the board. Since backgammon is basically a race, every time you hit one of your opponent's checkers, you put him further behind in the race. The closer a checker is to home, the more pips are lost when it is hit. Hitting a blot in your opponent's inner board (as in Position 1) is particularly good since that checker will lose many pips in making the journey around again. On the other hand, hitting a blot in *your* inner board is of limited value since that checker is already about as far back as it can be; a blot hit in your inner board doesn't lose much ground so far as the race is concerned.

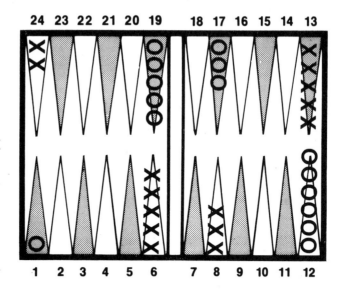

Position 4
X on Roll. What Does X
Need to Hit?

Conversely, you generally try to avoid being hit yourself. The closer a checker is to home, the more serious the loss of pips if hit. You lose a lot of ground if you are hit in your own inner board, whereas being hit in your opponent's inner board has little significance so far as the race is concerned.

You can never play completely safe even if you try to; leaving blots is inevitable and, as we shall see later, often desirable. Blots, however, must never be left needlessly. When you are forced to leave a blot, consider placing it where it is least likely to be hit and/or where the hit will cost you the least number of pips. You must be aware not only of what number you need to hit your opponent, but also to what numbers you, yourself, are exposed.

In Position 5 we see that X could hit on the one point with a 5. If X hit, however, his checker would then be in danger of being hit back by O as O re-enters from the bar. If X were hit, he would have to re-enter himself in O's

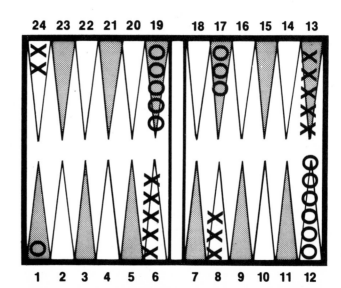

Position 5
X to Play 5–1

inner board. Because of this **return shot** (a shot which your opponent has back at you after you have hit him), X has little to gain but much to lose by such a hit. If X plays 13/8, 24/23, he leaves two men exposed in O's inner board. However, O has little to gain by hitting these blots.

Making Points

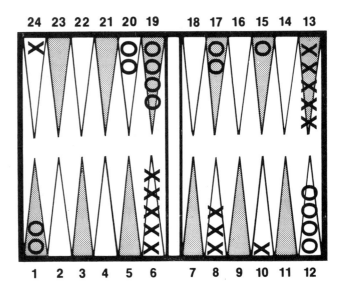

Position 6
X to Play 6–2

In order to avoid leaving blots, it is often necessary to bring two men together to **close** or **make points.** In Position 6, X can bring his blot to safety by playing 10/8, but then has no way to play his 6 without leaving a direct shot.

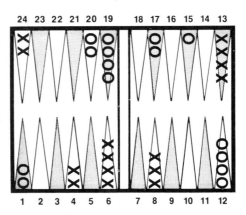

Position 6A
(X 6–2 10/4, 6/4)

The correct play is 10/4, 6/4 as seen in Position 6A. This play makes the four point. Before analyzing the benefits of making points, let's examine how to find plays that do make points.

In Position 6, the two men that came together to make the four point started out 4 pips apart on the six point and the ten point. A 6–2 was the number rolled; the difference between 6 and 2 is 4. Therefore, if we can find two checkers which are 4 pips apart they will end up on the same point, making that point. We move the man furthest away from the point to be made 6 pips, and the closer man 2 pips.

Let's look at another example:

Position 7
X to Play 6–3

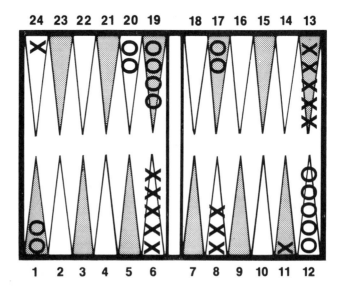

In Position 7, X has 6–3 to play. 6 minus 3=3; therefore, we look for two checkers which are 3 pips apart. We see that the men on the eight and eleven points are 3 pips apart so that they will come together on the five point. The correct move is 11/5, 8/5 as shown in Position 7A.

Position 7A
(X 6–3 11/5, 8/5)

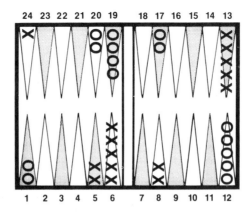

Let's look at Position 7 again. Assume that X has instead a 6–4 to play. 6 minus 4 = 2; therefore, two checkers which are 2 pips apart will end up on the same point. The men on the eight and six points are 2 pips apart. Thus we move 8/2, 6/2, making the two points as shown in Position 7B.

In Position 7, the men on the thirteen and eleven points are also 2 pips apart. If, with our roll of 6–4, we move 13/7, 11/7, as shown in Position 7C, we can make the **bar point.**

Position 7B
(X 6–4 8/2, 6/2)

Position 7C
(X 6–4 13/7, 11/7)

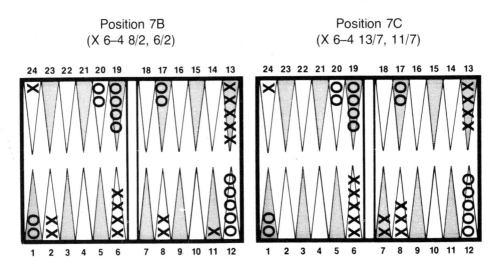

In Position 7, then, we have a choice of which point to make with a roll of 6–4. The relative value of each point will be discussed shortly.

Notice that while this "difference method" is the easiest way to search for ways in which to make new points with a particular roll, it does not automatically *create* new points.

Position 8
X to Play 3–1

Position 9
X to Play 3–1

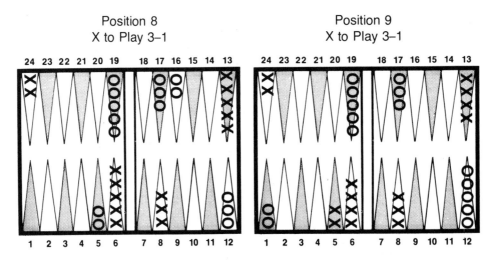

In Positions 8 and 9, X has 3–1 to play and in both cases there are men 2 pips apart on the six and eight points.

In the case of 8, you cannot create a *new* point since O already owns the five point. If O had a single man on the five point, X could make a point *on O's head* by hitting O and sending him to the bar.

In 9, X cannot create a new point since he already owns the five point.

Why do you want to make points?

In Position 6, you want to make your blots safe by making them into points. Already established points may also act as landing places to safely park your spare men. If you are short of points, you may be forced to expose men which you don't want hit. In Position 9, for example, X could play 6–2 safely by playing 13/5 and resting on the five point.

Another fundamental reason for creating points is to hinder your opponent's movement. Since your opponent cannot land on your points, every point you make restricts his choice of moves. Controlling three or more points in a row forms a blockade and makes it more difficult for your opponent to get past you.

These ideas will be illustrated and explained in later chapters. We advise you *first* to get out a backgammon set and follow along during the sample games. The best way to play with the book is to look at the dice roll and then try to make the moves yourself before looking at the answer. Better yet, get a friend to make all the moves for O while you play all the moves for X.

Summary

On every roll you will be faced with many possible legal plays. If you are a beginner, concentrate on the following *three primary goals* in considering your move. When you become more familiar with basic checker play, you will be in a good position to look at the strategic aspects of the game.

1. *Hit your opponent advantageously.* Sometimes a hit may not be advantageous — see Position 5.

2. *Play safely to avoid being hit.* Never leave men exposed to your opponent needlessly. When you do leave men exposed, leave the fewest possible direct shots. Avoid double or triple shots and leave indirect shots (7 pips or more away) in preference to direct shots.

3. *Make points.*

CHAPTER 4.
GAME I: RUNNING
GAME

EVERY GAME OF backgammon is essentially a race: the first person to success-fully move his men around the board and bear them off is the winner. However, if the game were just a race, then there would be little skill involved — the player rolling the higher numbers would win. This is not the case in backgammon. Because your opponent can block you by making points and you are always in danger of being hit, the game may be better thought of as an obstacle course.

Game I illustrates the basic strategy of safely navigating the obstacles and winning the race. It is called a **running game** because your primary strategy is to enter directly into a favorable race. Game I, as well as Game II, will be completely concerned with the play of the men, and thus the doubling cube will not be used.

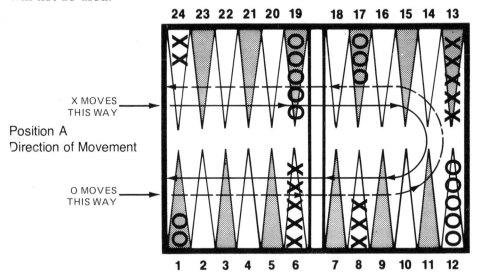

First, set up your checkers in the opening position (Position A). Remember that the direction of movement is indicated by the arrows in the diagram. Thus X moves from the twenty-four point around to the twelve point and over to the one point, while O moves in the opposite direction: from the one point to the thirteen point and then over to the twenty-four point.

On the opening roll, as stated in the rules, each player rolls one die. The player having the higher number moves first and must use for his first move the two numbers which have just been rolled.

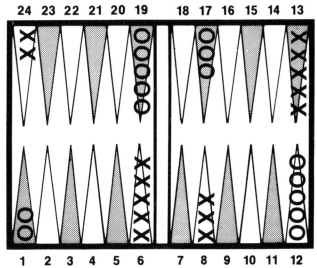

Roll 1
X 6, O 5, X to Play 6–5

The notation on the diagram above indicates that X has rolled a 6 and O, a 5. Therefore X takes the first move, 6–5. What are the possibilities for X? Try to make the move yourself before reading on.

The correct play is 24/13. This is indicated in the diagram below, O's Roll 2, where X 6–5 24/13 in parentheses indicates that X has already played his number. By moving one checker from the twenty-four point to the thirteen point, X begins to move the checkers that have the furthest to go in the circuit around the board. This is an important part of the opening strategy of the game. 6–5 is considered a good opening roll because it enables one **back man** to flee to complete safety.

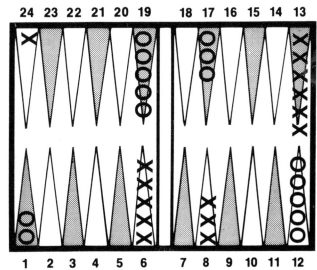

Roll 2 for O
O to Play 6–1
(X 6–5 24/13)

After the opening roll, players alternately roll both their dice to determine the move they will make. It is now O's turn. The diagram above indicates that, following X's opening move, O has rolled 6–1. How would you play this roll? Remember that O moves in the opposite direction from X.

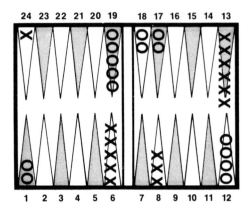

Correct Play: Roll 2 for O
(O 6–1 12/18, 17/18)

The correct play is 12/18, 17/18. The new point that O has made, the eighteen point, is called O's **bar point.** (Similarly, X's bar point would be the seven point.) The bar point is one of the most important points you can make at the beginning of the game. (Remembering our discussion in the previous chapter on the "difference method" of spotting rolls that make a point, we can see that 6–1 forms a point since 6 minus 1 = 5, and since the men on the twelve and seventeen points start 5 pips apart and thus go to the same place.)

Let's examine some alternate plays for O's roll of 6–1.

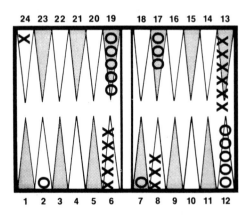

Alternate Move 1:
Roll 2 for O
(O 6–1 1/7, 1/2)

O can move 1/7, 1/2, as shown above to the left. Although O, following the logic of X's first move, would also like to begin to get his back men home, this move would leave the man on X's bar point exposed to a double direct shot.

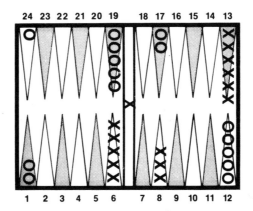

Alternate Move 2:
Roll 2 for O
(O 6–1 17/24*)

In the second alternate move, O can hit X by playing 17/24*. But, as pointed out in Chapter 3, O has little to gain by hitting on the twenty-four point since this move would expose O to a return shot by X's checker on the bar. If X re-enters on the one point hitting O, O will lose considerable ground in the race.

Let's return to the position after the correct move for O has been made.

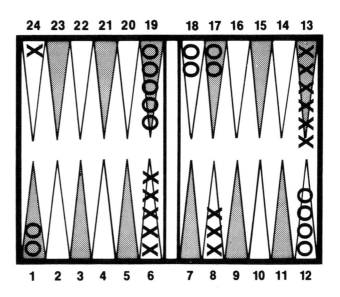

Roll 2 for X
X to Play 3–1
(O 6–1 12/18, 17/18)

X now has 3–1 to play. How would you play this move?

The correct play is 8/5, 6/5. (Again, by taking the difference of the numbers on the dice you can see that two men that start 2 pips apart will end up together on the same point.) The five point which we have made is also one of the most valuable points in the game. At the beginning of the game, you not only want to "escape" your back runners, but you also want to contain your opponent's back runners by making points in *front* of him.

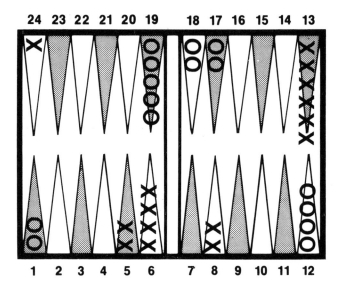

O's correct play of 5–4 in Roll 3 is 12/17, 12/16, shown below.

Correct Play: Roll 3 for O
(O 5–4 12/17, 12/16)

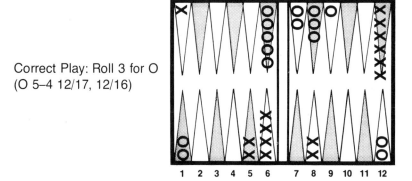

There is no "perfect play" for every roll in backgammon; you must often choose the best of several possible moves, or one which does nothing spectacular but isn't as harmful as another. Although this play exposes a man to an indirect shot (an 8), any other play would leave a *direct* shot (6 pips or less away), which is far more likely to be hit. (Remember that X's men on the thirteen point do not threaten your blot, since they cannot move backward.)

Let's look at some alternate plays.

Alternate Move 1:
Roll 3 for O
(O 5–4 1/10)

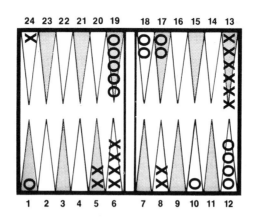

Alternate Move 2:
Roll 3 for O
(O 5–4 19/24*, 12/16)

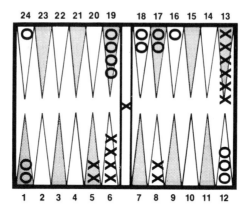

The first alternate move, 1/10, is not legal. Remember that the numbers on the dice have to be taken *separately;* you cannot simply hop to the point corresponding to the sum of the two numbers. Since X has covered both the six and five points, neither the 4 nor 5 on the dice may be legally moved from the one point.

The second alternate move is 19/24*, 12/16. This hit exposes O to a return shot and thus a considerable loss of pips.

Alternate Move 3:
Roll 3 for O
(O 5–4 17/22, 18/22)

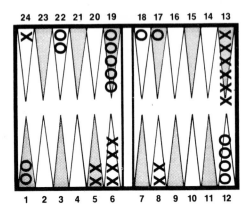

The third alternate move is 17/22, 18/22. You may have noticed that, since the difference in the two numbers on the dice is 1 (5 minus 4=1), a new point can be made by moving one checker from the seventeen and one from the eighteen points which are 1 pip apart. However, there are two drawbacks to creating the twenty-two point: First of all, you are making one new point at the expense of giving up two other points (the seventeen and eighteen), which are more valuable. Secondly, by making the twenty-two point you expose yourself to a direct shot, 6, and an indirect shot, 7. If either of these men are hit, they will have to start back again in X's inner board. It is important to be aware of the hitting possibilities that your opponent will have as a result of your own play.

Let's go back to the position after the correct move for O has been played.

Roll 3 for X
X to Play 5–5
(O 5–4 12/17, 12/16)

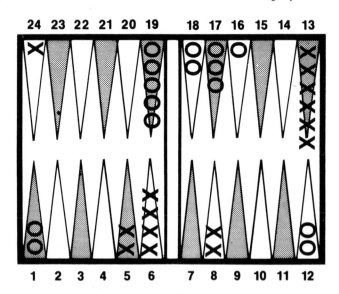

X has now rolled double 5's and has four 5's to play.

The correct move is 13/3 (2). Since X's back man cannot escape with a 5, X makes another point in front of O to block O's back men.

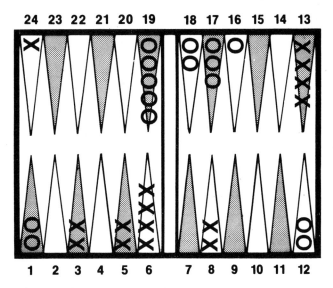

Roll 4 for O
O to Play 5–2
(X 5–5 13/3[2])

By correctly moving 16/21, 19/21, O can make a valuable point, the twenty-one point. O also **safeties** his man who was on the sixteen point; by **safety** we mean bringing a blot to a position where it cannot be hit. Another advantage of this move is that by making the twenty-one point, O is now beginning to seriously impede X's escape from the twenty-four point.

Remember, the difference method may help you find ways to make new points. If we look at O's last roll, 5–2, we can see that 5 minus 2 = 3. Therefore, in order for two checkers to make a point in this position, they must initially start 3 pips apart.

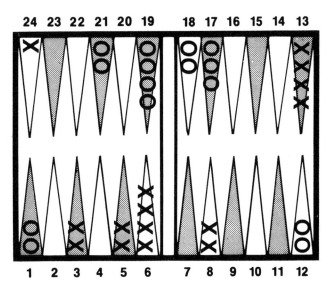

Roll 4 for X
X to Play 6–2
(O 5–2 16/21, 19/21)

The correct play is 24/16. X is beginning to feel trapped and seizes this opportunity to make a run for it. This is a calculated risk since the back   is exposed to a direct 4-shot.

A possible alternate move would be to play it safe by moving 13/5. This play is sound; however, in this case, the advantage of escaping a second back man is worth the risk of even a direct shot that would send the escapee back 8 pips.

Roll 5 for O
O to Play 4–2
(X 6–2 24/16)

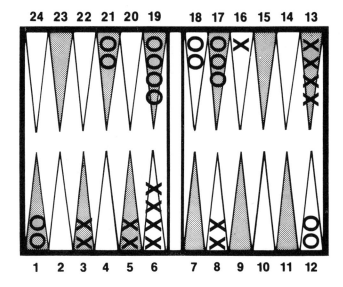

The correct play is to bring two men down from the twelve point: 12/16* (hitting the blot), 12/14. It is fortunate for O that he hit X since otherwise X might have been able to complete his escape.

Correct Play: Roll 5 for O
(O 4–2 12/16*, 12/14)

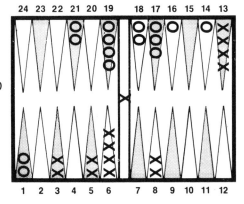

An alternate play would be to move 12/16*/18.

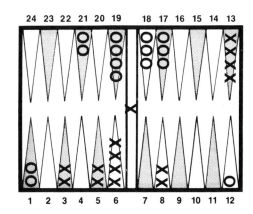

Alternate Move:
Roll 5 for O
(O 4–2 12/16*/18)

Although this move might appear safer than the correct play since it leaves only one blot on the twelve point (instead of two blots — on the fourteen and sixteen points), that one blot would be exposed to a direct 1-shot from the men on the thirteen point. By correctly playing 12/16*, 12/14, O is not exposed·to any direct shots since the men on the thirteen point cannot move backward. Even several indirect shots are often less likely to be hit than a single direct shot.

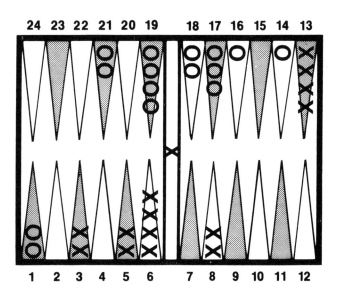

Roll 5 for X
X to Play 4–3
(O 4–2 12/16*, 12/14)

Before we discuss this play, remember that according to the rules a player may not move *any* men until all his checkers on the bar have been re-entered in his opponent's home board. You must re-enter with a number that corresponds to an open point in your opponent's home board. Here a 1 on the dice corresponds to the first point in O's home board, the twenty-four point; 2 to the twenty-three point; 3, the twenty-two point, etc.

In this position, the twenty-four, twenty-three, twenty-two, and twenty points are open; the twenty-one and nineteen points are closed. If X rolls 6–4 in this position he would be unable to re-enter and would forfeit his turn.

X's correct play for 4–3 is bar/22, 13/9. X *must* come in on the twenty-two point with the 3 since the twenty-one point is closed (corresponding to the 4 on the dice). Playing 13/9 leaves an indirect shot, but it is the safest move possible in this position. Taking any other 4, such as 8/4 or 6/2, would leave a direct shot.

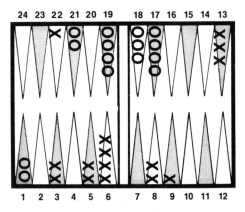

Roll 6 for O
O to Play 4–1
(X 4–3 bar/22, 13/9)

The correct play is 16/20, 19/20, making the twenty point. You now have several points in a row forming a blockade in front of X's back man. It is very hard for X to escape from behind five points in a row. X needs at least a specific 6 on the dice to escape.

An alternate move for O would be 16/17, 14/18.

Alternate Move:
Roll 6 for O
(O 4–1 14/18, 16/17)

This play leaves no man exposed but fails to make the twenty point. The correct play leaves one man exposed to an indirect shot, an 8. The only number which could possibly hit in this case is 6–2, so the risk is minimal.

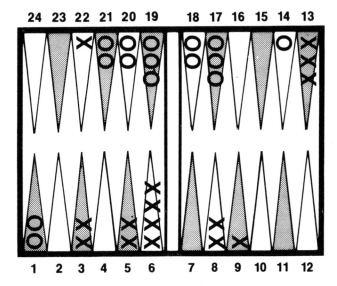

Roll 6 for X
X to Play 6–4
(O 4–1 16/20, 19/20)

The correct play is 22/12.

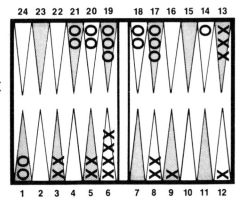

Correct Play: Roll 6 for X
(X 6–4 22/12)

X rolls the vital 6 and escapes.
    An alternate play is 8/2, 6/2.

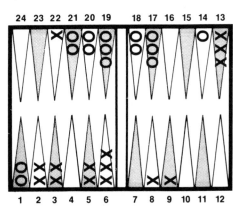

Alternate Move 1:
Roll 6 for X
(X 6–4 8/2, 6/2)

This move makes the two point in front of O's back men. It is more important, however, to escape from O's inner board.

Another alternate play is 22/16, 13/9.

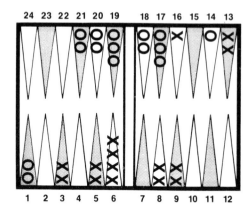

Alternate Move 2:
Roll 6 for X
(X 6–4 22/16, 13/9)

This play leaves you exposed to one direct 2-shot. The correct play leaves you exposed to two indirect shots, 8 and 11, but this single shot is twice as likely to be hit as both indirect shots, so we reject this play.

Let's stop for a moment and assess the position: Despite O's efforts, X has escaped both back men and is well ahead in the race because of the 5–5 which X rolled earlier. Both of O's back men are still in X's inner board. X, therefore, has a significant advantage at this time.

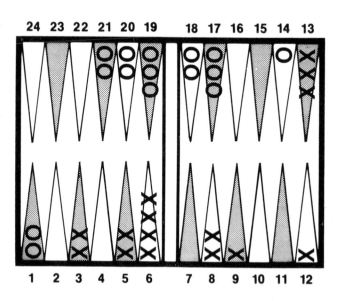

Roll 7 for O
O to Play 6–6
(X 6–4 22/12)

To return to the game, O is on roll and rolls 6–6.

The correct play is 1/7(2), 17/23(2). O seizes the opportunity to bring both his back men out safely to X's bar point (the seven point). The second part of the move, 17/23(2), establishes a new point in O's inner board. O doesn't worry about the blots he leaves on the seventeen and fourteen points since these men are not exposed to any of X's checkers.

O's strategy at this time is to hope to hit X as X comes home. The more closed points O has in his inner board, the harder it will be for X to re-enter if he is hit. If X is hit now, only two numbers, 1 and 3, will allow him to re-enter.

If O were able to close *all* his inner-board points, he would have a **closed board.** If X were then hit, he would be unable to re-enter and would forfeit all his turns, remaining on the bar, until O opened one of his inner-board points. Therefore, one basic strategy in backgammon is to close as many inner-board points as possible to make the position dangerous for your opponent if he is hit.

Roll 7 for X
X to Play 5–3
(O 6–6 1/7 [2], 17/23 [2])

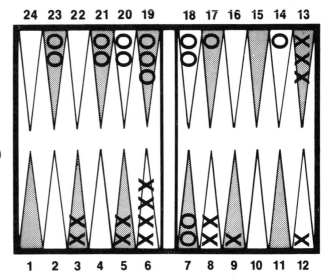

X correctly moves 13/8, 12/9. With a single number, 3, X safeties both his blots and avoids the danger of being hit.

Roll 8 for O
O to Play 5–4
(X 5–3 13/8, 12/9)

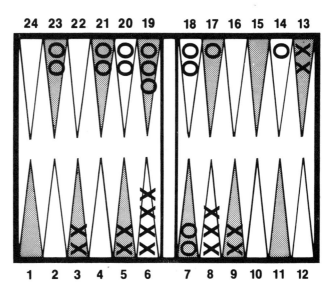

The correct play is 17/22, 18/22. O closes another inner-board point. He cannot bring his two back men on the seven point closer to home without exposing himself to a double or triple shot.

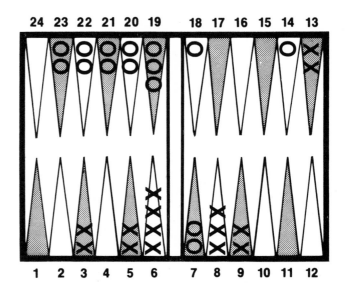

Roll 8 for X
X to Play 4–4
(O 5–4 17/22, 18/22)

The correct play is 13/5(2). X moves his men closer to home. He is still ahead in the race.

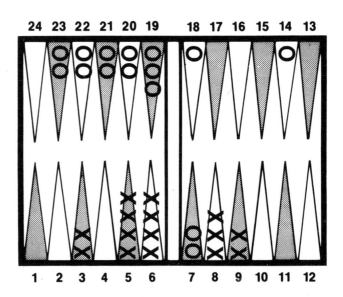

Roll 9 for O
O to Play 3–1
(X 4–4 13/5 [2])

The correct play is 14/17, 18/19. The object of the game is to bring all your men around the board and into your inner board in preparation for the bear-off. Remember, the bear-off process may not begin until you have *all* your men in your inner board. This is why O brings one man in and another closer to his inner board.

Roll 9 for X
X to Play 5–4
(O 3–1 14/17, 18/19)

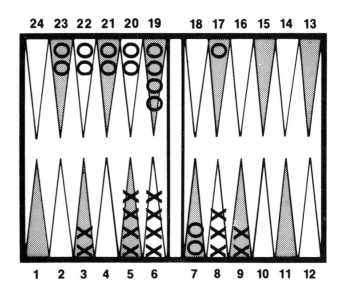

The correct play is 9/4, 9/5. X brings two men into his inner board. He does not make his one point since, in this position, little contact is likely, and the game is basically a race. The player who rolls the higher numbers and gets off the board first will win.

Roll 10 for O
O to Play 6–4
(X 5–4 9/4, 9/5)

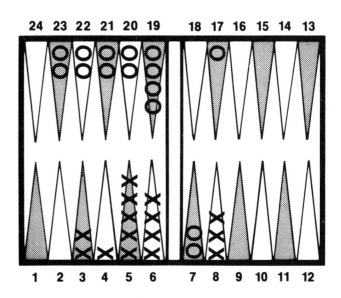

The correct play is 7/13, 7/11. O brings his two rearmost men closer to home. Even though he is behind in the race, there is no reason to remain on X's bar point since there is no longer any real prospect of hitting X.

Roll 10 for X
X to Play 5–4
(O 6–4 7/13, 7/11)

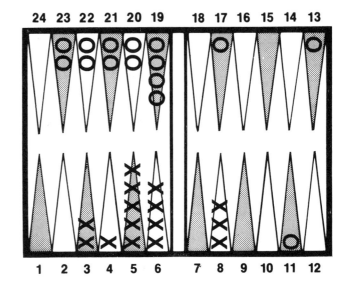

The correct play is 8/3, 8/4. X continues bringing his men into his inner board as quickly as possible. Since the game is now completely a race and no further contact is possible, the players do not have to worry about exposed checkers.

Roll 11 for O
O to Play 4–3
(X 5–4 8/3. 8/4)

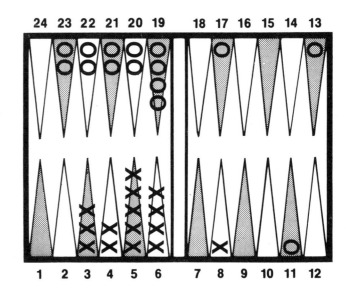

The correct play is 11/15, 17/20. O moves closer to home.

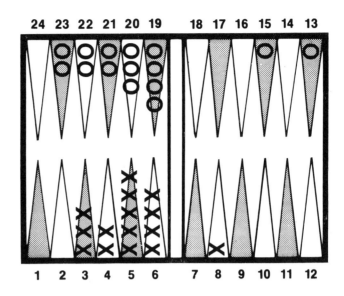

Roll 11 for X
X to Play 4–1
(O 4–3 11/15, 17/20)

The correct play is 8/4, 3/2. X brings one checker into his inner board and moves another on to an empty point in preparation for bearing off.

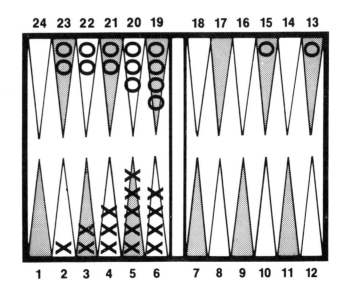

Roll 12 for O
O to Play 5–3
(X 4–1 8/4, 3/2)

O moves 15/20, 13/16 closer to his home board.

It is now X's roll. On his last move he completed bringing all his men into his inner board. He may now begin the bear-off process. The ultimate objective of the game is to bear all your men off the board before your opponent does so. Remember that each number rolled may be used to bear off a man from the corresponding point. Thus, the most economical way to bear off is to use one number on the dice for each bear-off — 3, for example, to take a man off the third point in your inner board. You can also move your checkers to unoccupied points within your inner board. 2–1 (when there are no checkers on either the two or one point) can be used to move a checker from the three point to either the two or one point, and thence off the board.

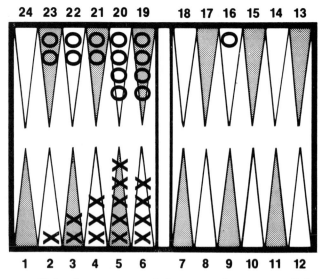

Roll 12 for X
X to Play 5–4
(O 5–3 15/20, 13/16)

X uses his 5 to take a man off the five point and the   to take a man off the four point: 5/off, 4/off. You want to take off as many men as possible on each roll. These men go off the board and remain permanently out of the game.

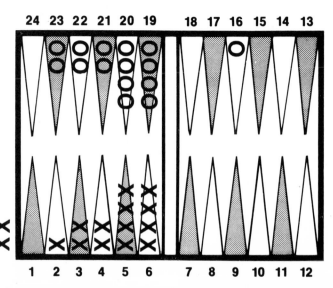

Roll 13 for O
O to Play 6–2
(X 5–4 5/off, 4/off)

O brings the last man in and begins bearing off by moving 16/22, 23/off.

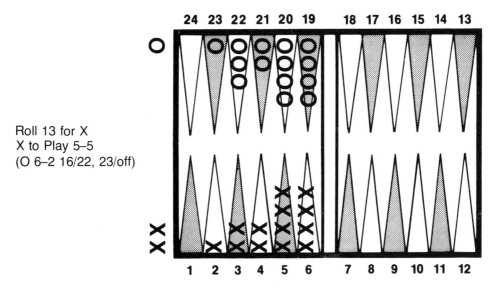

Roll 13 for X
X to Play 5–5
(O 6–2 16/22, 23/off)

Doubles can be especially effective in the bear-off process. X correctly takes his four 5's off the five point: 5/off (4).

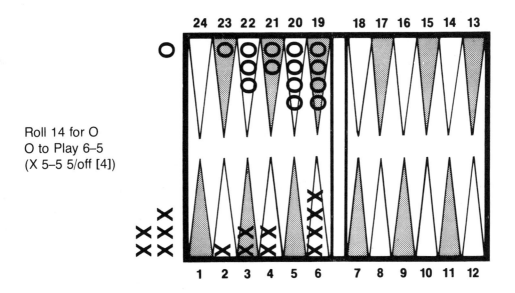

Roll 14 for O
O to Play 6–5
(X 5–5 5/off [4])

O moves 19/off, 20/off.

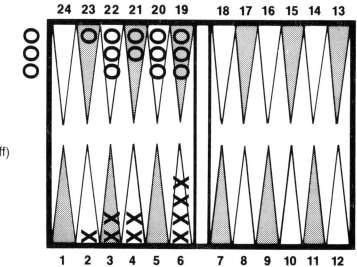

Roll 14 for X
X to Play 6–1
(O 6–5 19/off, 20/off)

X correctly plays 6/off, 6/5. Since X cannot take any men off with the 1, he moves a checker to an empty point so as to increase the possible number of bear-offs on the next roll. When you cannot take a checker off, try to fill up gaps.

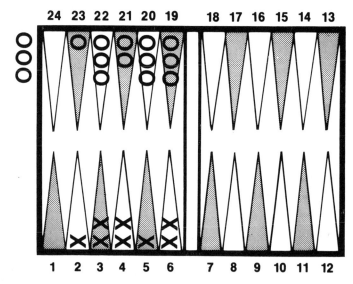

Roll 15 for O
O to Play 3–3
(X 6–1 6/off, 6/5)

O plays 22/off(3), 19/22. After taking three men off the twenty–two point, the fourth 3 is played to fill the empty point, or gap.

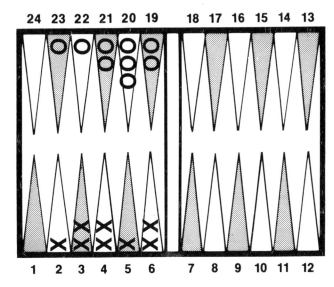

Roll 15 for X
X to Play 4–3
(O 3–3 22/off [3], 19/22)

X plays 4/off, 3/off.

In the next five moves, each player bears off as many men as possible. Diagrams are omitted until Roll 18 for X.

Roll 16 for O: O rolls 5–4. O plays 20/off, 21/off.
Roll 16 for X: X rolls 6–3. X plays 6/off, 3/off.
Roll 17 for O: O rolls 5–2. O plays 20/off, 23/off.
Roll 17 for X: X rolls 6–2. X plays 6/off., 2/off.
Roll 18 for O: O rolls 5–4. O plays 20/off, 21/off.

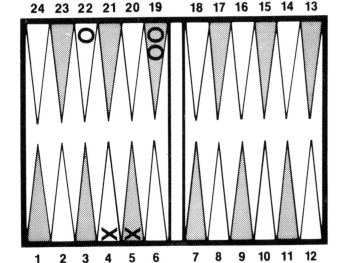

Roll 18 for X
X to Play 6–1
(O 5–4 20/off, 21/off)

Remember that if a player rolls a number higher than the furthest point from "off" on which a checker rests, the checker on the *next-highest* point must be taken off instead.

X plays 5/off, 4/3. By moving the last checker to the three point, he insures getting off on his next turn since any roll will be sufficient to do so.

In order for O to win now, he must bear off all three of his men on this roll. This can only be done with 6–6.

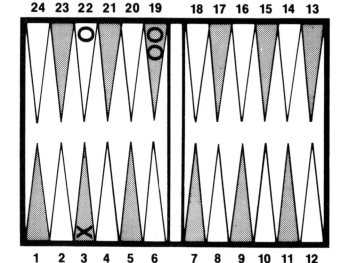

Roll 19 for O
O to Play 5–4
(X 6–1 5/off, 4/3)

Unfortunately, O does not roll the needed 6–6. Having failed to do so, he would actually concede the game now. However, we shall play out the move to make the bear-off rules clear.

O moves 19/24, 19/23. O may not use either the 5 or the 4 to bear the man off the twenty-two point, despite the fact that the twenty and twenty-one points are empty. In backgammon you must take the *full* number whenever possible. Only if there is no man on a higher-numbered point than the number rolled can you take a man off the next-lowest point than the number rolled. Here the 5 and 4 *must* be played from the nineteen point.

If O, on the other hand, had men only on the twenty-two point, then the 5–4 could be used to bear two men off.

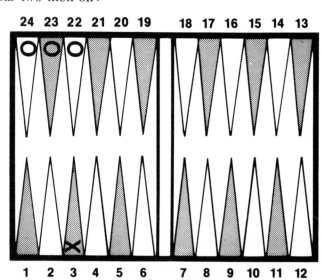

Roll 19 for X
X to Play Anything
(O 5–4 19/24, 19/23)

Any roll wins for X. He automatically bears off his last man and wins the game.

Game I — Summary of Ideas

Initial Strategy

A. Start to move your back men because they have the furthest to go.

B. Try to contain your opponent's back men.

Middle Game

A. Avoid being hit. Since backgammon is a race, men should never be exposed needlessly — any man hit loses ground in the race. The closer a man is to your home board, the more ground he has to lose, and the more careful you should be about leaving him exposed.

B. Try to hit your opponent. However, be aware of possible **return shots.** In particular, hitting in your home board and leaving a blot risks losing ground in the race if that blot is subsequently hit.

C. Direct vs. indirect shots: When leaving men exposed, try to leave them 7 or more pips away (an indirect shot) rather than 6 or less pips away (direct shot) from your opponent. In that way you considerably minimize your chances of being hit.

D. Taking strategic risks: The safest possible play is not always the most strategic play. For example, in Roll 4, X left his back man exposed to a direct shot in order to escape from O's inner board; in Roll 6, O left a man indirectly exposed so that he could make a vital point to block X in his inner board.

E. Making points: This is one of the chief objectives of the game (see Basic Checker Play, page 24, for hints on how to recognize when it is possible to make new points). By making points: 1. You bring men together, removing blots and making safe places for future men to land; 2. You block your opponent and hinder his movement — especially if you form several points in a row to form a blockade; 3. You hinder his re-entry in your inner board should he be hit. The more inner-board points you are able to close, the harder it will be for your opponent to re-enter.

Bearing Off

Try to bear off as many men as possible as soon as possible. If you cannot take a checker off, move to fill up gaps so that future rolls offer more opportunities to bear men off.

CHAPTER 5.
OPENING ROLLS

A KNOWLEDGE OF the standard opening moves and the reasons for making them is essential to mastering backgammon. If you are a new player, spend some time studying the opening moves. They should become second nature after several games. There are alternate opening moves available to more experienced players. These are discussed *Backgammon* (page 204).

For convenience we will divide the opening rolls into groups.

Closing Strategic Points

The beginning of the game is essentially a two-fold struggle: extricating your back checkers and, by closing points on your side, trapping O's checkers. The order in which you close points to contain O is important. The most valuable points to close first are your *five* point, *bar* point (seven point), and *four* point in that order. The best opening rolls are those that enable you to make these points immediately: 3–1, 6–1, 4–2.

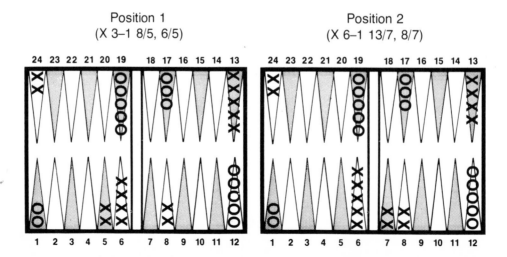

Position 1
(X 3–1 8/5, 6/5)

Position 2
(X 6–1 13/7, 8/7)

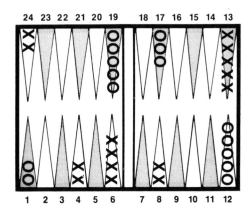

Position 3
(X 4–2 8/4, 6/4)

Bringing Checkers from the Midpoint as Builders

In order to increase the chance of forming these key points (five, bar, four), it is necessary to have spare men or **builders** to bear upon these points. Points do not form automatically; you have to work to make them. For this reason, the concept of builders is extremely important. The following group of moves enables you to bring checkers down from the midpoint (thirteen point of player moving the checkers) into the outer board as builders: 5–4, 4–3, 5–2, 5–3, 3–2.

Position 4
(X 5–4 13/8, 13/9)

Position 5
(X 4–3 13/9, 13/10)

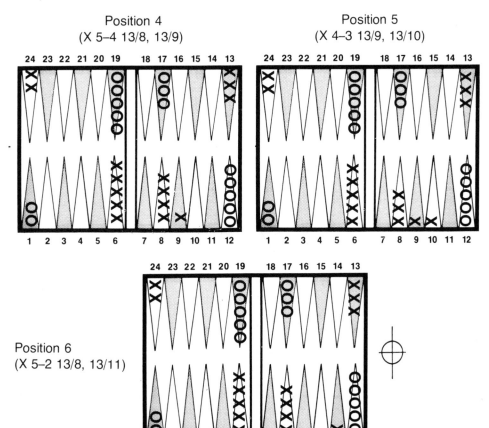

Position 6
(X 5–2 13/8, 13/11)

Position 7
(X 5–3 13/8, 13/10)

Position 8
(X 3–2 13/10, 13/11)

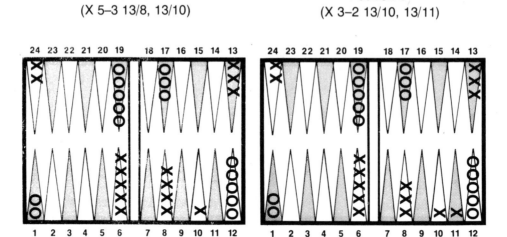

Note that 4–3, 5–3, 5–2, 3–2 could be played safely without leaving any blots. However, the value of the builders created by the indicated plays more than offsets the danger of being hit by certain indirect shots.

5–3 could also be used to make the three point. However, despite the importance of making points in your home board, deep points — namely the three, two, and especially the one — are not effective in blocking opposing checkers unless the intervening four and five points have already been made. Closing these deep points takes checkers out of play that may be used more constructively elsewhere.

Running with One Back Man

The third group of rolls does not enable you to safely make useful points or create builders, use them to begin to extricate your own back men: 6–5, 6–4, 6–2, 6–3.

Position 9
(X 6–5 24/13)

Position 10
(X 6–4 24/14)

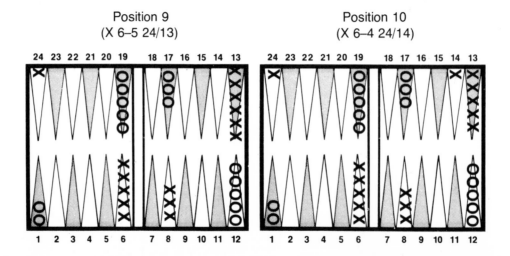

Position 11
(X 6–2 24/16)

Position 12
(X 6–3 24/15)

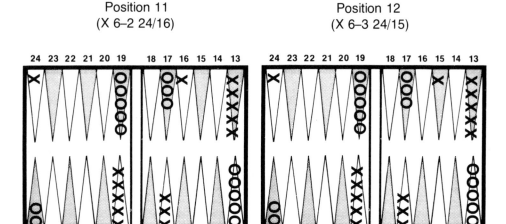

With each of these moves you run a back checker to O's outer board. The 6–5 move goes to the midpoint. There is no safe way to play the other numbers, but, if the checker escapes being hit, you will have only one checker remaining in O's home board.

Although 6–4 could make the two point, this is definitely inadvisable since the two point is too far advanced to have much blocking potential.

Creating a Builder and Splitting Your Back Men

In this last group you play the higher number from the midpoint into your outer board and split the back checkers by moving one of them to the twenty-three point. Splitting the back checkers facilitates their escape at small risk since O gains little by hitting on a point deep in his inner board: 4–1, 2–1, 5–1.

Position 13
(X 4–1 13/9, 24/23)

Position 14
(X 2–1 13/11, 24/23)

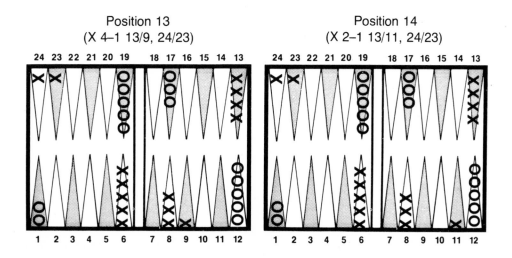

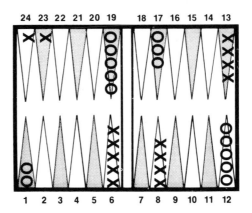

Position 15
(X 5–1 13/8, 24/23)

Rolling Doubles

Since play begins with each player rolling one die, and ties are re-thrown, doubles can never be the opening roll of the game. The standard first moves for double rolls are listed below. Bear in mind that variations may have to be used, depending upon your opponent's opening move.

6–6: Close your opponent's bar point and your own bar point.

5–5: Move two checkers from your midpoint to the three point.

Position 16   Position 17
(X 6–6 24/18 [2], 13/7 [2])   (X 5–5 13/3 [2])

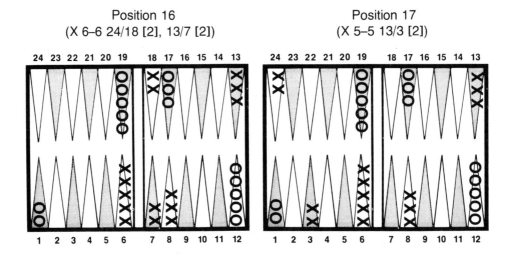

4–4: Close the twenty point and the nine point.

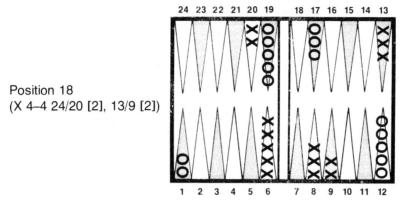

Position 18
(X 4–4 24/20 [2], 13/9 [2])

The twenty point (O's five point) has tremendous defensive value for you. It is probably the single most important point in the game. Controlling this point gives you a measure of security throughout the game by providing you with a direct shot at any blot in your opponent's outer board, by making it difficult for your opponent to block these checkers behind a prime, and by providing you with a secure entry point should you be hit.

3–3: Close the twenty-one point and the five point. The twenty-one point has a strategic value similar to the twenty point.

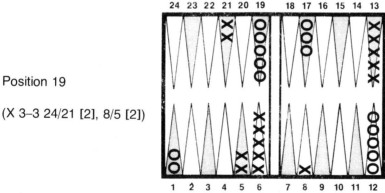

Position 19

(X 3–3 24/21 [2], 8/5 [2])

2–2: Close the twenty point. Another strong play would be to close the eleven and four points.

Position 20
(X 2–2 24/20 [2])

Position 20A
(X 2–2 13/11 [2], 6/4 [2])

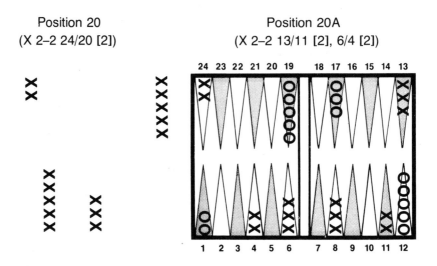

1–1: Close your bar point (seven point) and five point.

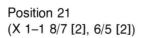

Position 21
(X 1–1 8/7 [2], 6/5 [2])

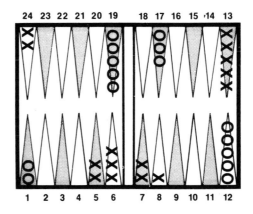

CHAPTER 6.
GAME II: HOLDING GAME

GAME II IS an example of a different type of game from a running game — a **holding game.** A holding game is characterized by holding a point or points in your opponent's inner and/or outer boards, hoping to hit him as he comes home. Unlike the running game, in a holding game a player can be way behind in the race and still win.

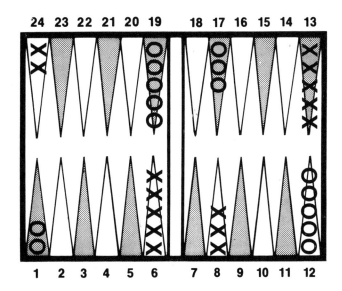

Roll 1
X 6, O 4, X to Play 6–4

X has won the first roll and has a 6–4 to play. What is your move?

X moves 24/14 as seen in Roll 2 for O, escaping with one of his back men but leaving that man exposed to a direct 2-shot.

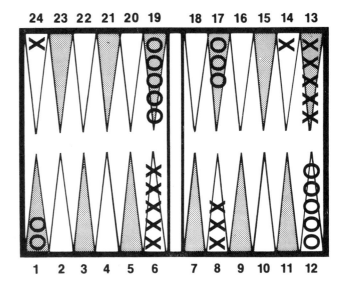

Roll 2 for O
O to Play 3–1
(X 6–4 24/14)

It is now O's turn. O chooses to make the key twenty point (O's five point) 19/20, 17/20. He would have liked to hit X but is unable to.

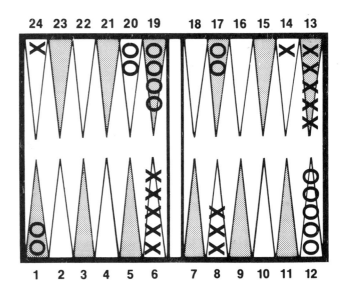

Roll 2 for X
X to Play 6–2
(O 3–1 19/20, 17/20)

X moves 14/8, bringing his blot to safety, and 24/22 to begin moving the remaining back man out of O's inner board. Another good alternate move would be 14/8, 13/11, safetying the blot and bringing a builder down from his midpoint. This builder greatly increases X's chance of making the five or bar point.

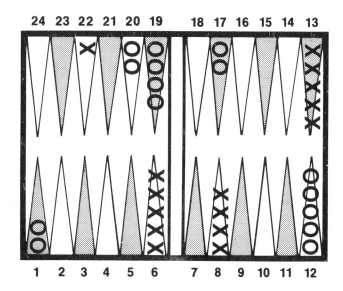

Roll 3 for O
O to Play 6–3
(X 6–2 14/8, 24/22)

O moves 1/10, trying to run. Hitting X on the twenty-two point is not advisable since X would then have a return shot which would send the O checker all the way back to X's inner board.

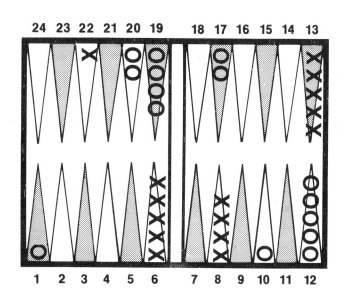

Roll 3 for X
X to Play 5–3
(O 6–3 1/10)

X moves 13/10*, hitting O's blot, and 13/8 bringing a man down safely from the midpoint.

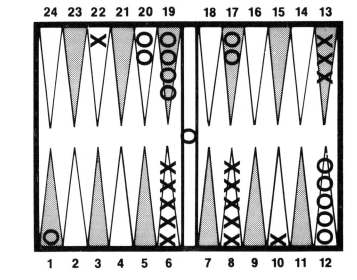

Roll 4 for O
O to Play 4–3
(X 5–3 13/10*, 13/8)

O moves bar/4, 1/4. This move brings in the checker from the bar, safeties both blots, and brings them closer to home. O has established a point in X's inner board called an **anchor**.

Whenever a player makes his opponent's four or five point, this is called making an **advanced anchor**. Holding such an advanced anchor is an extremely important strategic objective since it affords a great amount of protection and security. The importance of such a point is underscored by the fact that it is preferable even to the player's own four or five point.

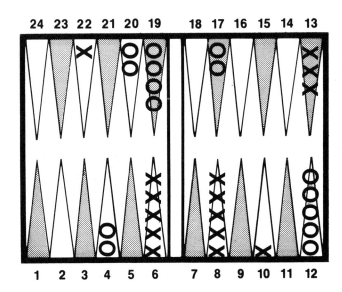

Roll 4 for X
X to Play 6–6
(O 4–3 bar/4, 1/4)

X moves 22/10, 8/2(2).

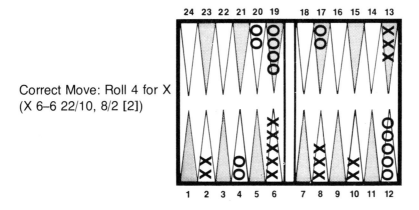

Correct Move: Roll 4 for X
(X 6–6 22/10, 8/2 [2])

X escapes completely from O's inner board and makes a new point in his own inner board. By making the ten point, you make it harder for O to escape his back men from the four point. As a general rule, if your opponent has a point in your inner board, the single most effective blocking point is the one which is 6 (or sometimes 5) pips in front of the opponent-held point.

Alternate Move 1 — 22/10, 13/1 — is also safe but does not make an inner-board point.

Alternate Move 2 — 22/10, 13/7(2) — makes the valuable bar point, which will serve as an effective landing spot to bring X's remaining checker home safely. The drawback in making this play is that it leaves X exposed to a direct 1-shot.

Alternate Move 1: Roll 4 for X   Alternate Move 2: Roll 4 for X
    (X 6–6 22/10, 13/1)   (X 6–6 22/10, 13/7 [2])

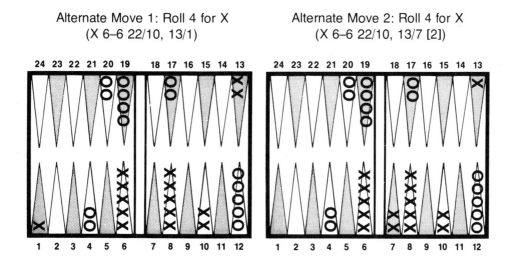

Before continuing Game II, let's assess the position. X has escaped both his back men and is ahead in the race because of the 6–6 he rolled. If X can come the rest of the way home safely, he will win the game. O's only chance is to hold X's four point and hope that X will have to leave a blot for O to hit.

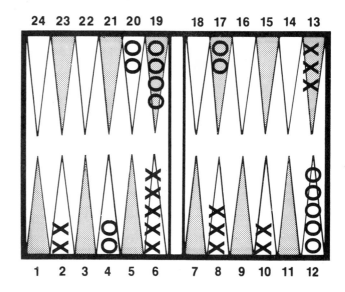

Roll 5 for O
O to Play 4–2
(X 6–6 22/10, 8/2 [2])

O moves 17/21, 19/21, making the valuable twenty-one point. According to the game plan outlined above, O hopes to get the chance to hit a shot. In preparation for this, he wants to rapidly close as many points in his own inner board as possible.

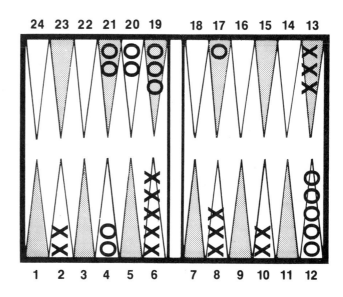

Roll 5 for X
X to Play 6–5
(O 4–2 17/21, 19/21)

X moves one checker 13/2. He does not want to leave any shots for O. X brings a man down from the thirteen point in preparation for **clearing** (removing all the checkers from) this point.

An alternate move for X is 8/2, 6/1. This is also safe but leaves an extra man on the thirteen point.

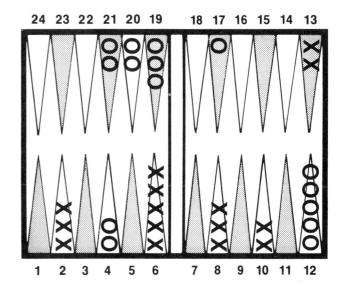

Roll 6 for O
O to Play 6–2
(X 6–5 13/2)

O moves 12/18, 12/14, bringing two builders down in preparation for making the bar point or another **inside point** (a point in his inner board). Note that despite O's three blots there is no danger involved in this move since X is not in a position to hit any of these blots.

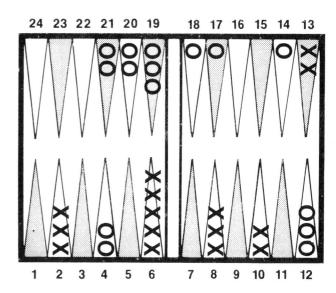

Roll 6 for X
X to Play 5–1
(O 6–2 12/18, 12/14)

X correctly moves 6/1, 2/1. X would like to make the five point with 10/5, 6/5, but this would leave him exposed to a direct shot. Similarly, bringing a man down from the midpoint with 13/8 would leave the remaining man on the midpoint exposed.

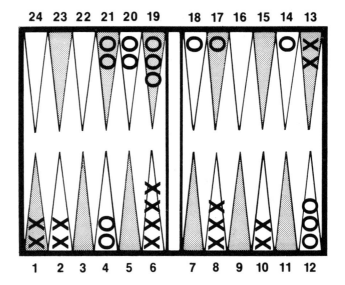

Roll 7 for O
O to Play 6–5
(X 5–1 6/1, 2/1)

O moves 17/23, 18/23, making another inner-board point and still hoping to hit X. Every new point closed in his inner board makes the position more perilous for his opponent since re-entry from the bar becomes more difficult. Remember that O's basic strategy at this time is to prevent X from getting home safely since O is behind in the race.

By remaining on the four point and twelve point (O's midpoint), O makes it hard for X to avoid leaving a shot as he comes home. For this reason O is playing a "holding game."

O has no guarantee that his holding game will be effective. X may be able to get home without leaving any shots, or X may leave a shot which O might miss. In some cases a well-played holding game will be an overwhelming favorite to win. In the present game O should not be considered a favorite, but nevertheless he pursues his most rational method of winning. It is important to play correctly in poor positions, giving yourself every possible opportunity to win.

An alternate move for O would be 12/18, 12/17.

This move would give O five consecutive points, a strong position. However,

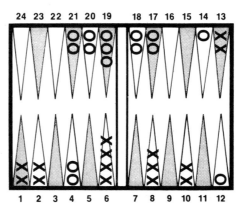

Alternate Move:
Roll 7 for O
(O 6–5 12/18, 12/17)

O would be giving up his midpoint and leaving a checker exposed to a direct shot in the process.

The midpoint has strategic value in itself which is often overlooked. In this holding game O's midpoint helps restrain the men on X's midpoint. If X wishes to move his last two men off the midpoint, he must wait until he rolls a number that enables him to bring *both* men down simultaneously; a single man left on the midpoint would be exposed to a direct 1-shot.

On the other hand, if O did not own his own midpoint, X would be able to clear his midpoint one checker at a time, leaving himself exposed to only an indirect 9-shot from O's checkers on the four point. O's midpoint has much more holding power than would appear since the majority of rolls do not permit X to safely bring both his men down simultaneously.

Roll 7 for X
X to Play 2–2
(O 6–5 17/23, 18/23)

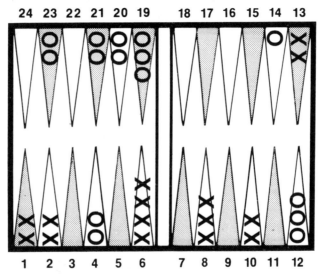

X moves 13/9(2), clearing his midpoint and further blocking O's back men. Owning the nine and ten points most effectively blocks the men on the four point.

An alternate move would be 13/11(2), 10/8(2).

Alternate Move:
Roll 7 for X
(X 2–2 13/11 [2], 10/8 [2])

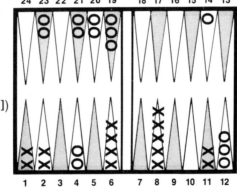

This play also clears the midpoint but does not effectively block O's men. However, in this position, with X ahead in the race, X is more concerned with bringing his men home safely than blocking O. For this reason the alternate move would be superior in an actual game; we use the inferior move here simply to illustrate holding-game tactics.

Roll 8 for O
O to Play 4–3
(X 2–2 13/9 [2])

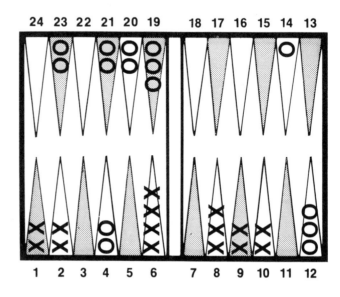

O moves 12/16, 14/17. O next wants to make the twenty-two point, so he brings two new builders to bear upon this point.

Roll 8 for X
X to Play 6–2
(O 4–3 12/16, 14/17)

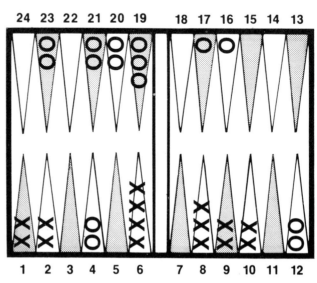

X moves 10/2. This is an unfortunate roll for X because there is no way he can avoid leaving a direct shot. When merely trying to get home safely, you should clear your points starting with the outermost ones first and working down to avoid leaving gaps. Since X has to leave a shot anyway, he takes this opportunity to begin to clear the ten point.

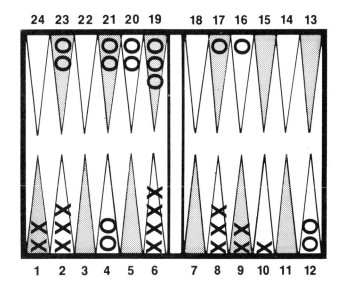

Roll 9 for O
O to Play 6–5
(X 6–2 10/2)

O jubilantly moves 4/10*, hitting X's blot, and 12/17, covering the seventeen point.

Despite the fact that enormous skill and complex decisions are involved in backgammon, many positions come down to the luck of hitting or missing a single shot. Thus the greatest players may be subject to unfortunate rolls, while the new player can defeat a more experienced player if he rolls the right numbers. This is one reason that backgammon is such a fascinating game; unexpected changes of fortune can affect the best players, although careful play can reduce the possibilities for disaster.

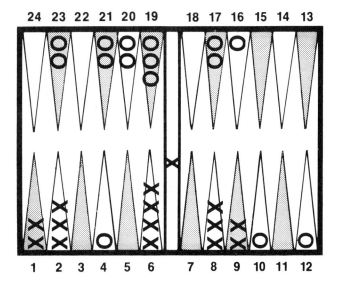

Roll 9 for X
X to Play 5–2
(O 6–5 4/10*, 12/17)

The symbol ø means that X can't move. Both the twenty-three and twenty points are covered so that X cannot re-enter with his roll of 5–2. X's checker remains on the bar, and X forfeits his turn since he is not permitted to make any other move until he has re-entered all his men.

In addition to being lucky in hitting X, O's last few moves have paid off. He had carefully built up his inner board in preparation for such a possibility.

Roll 10 for O
O to Play 3–3
(X 5–2 φ)

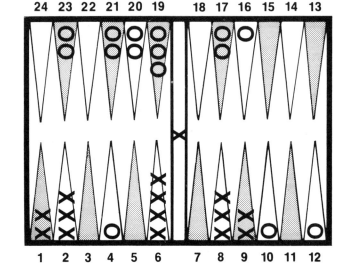

O moves 16/22, 19/22, covering the twenty-two point, and 17/20 bringing a builder in to bear upon the last open point (the twenty-four point). X now must roll a 1 to re-enter.

Again we point out how rapidly the game has changed. Two rolls ago, X was far ahead in the race, with matters seemingly well in hand. Now X is in a desperate position on the bar against a 5-point board, and even if he does re-enter he will be behind a 5-point prime.

Backgammon is much more than a simple racing game: It is a game of position and strategy. As we study Games III and IV, we shall see other game plans for winning besides merely getting ahead and staying ahead in the race.

Roll 10 for X
X to Play 3–1
(O 3–3 16/22,
19/22, 17/20)

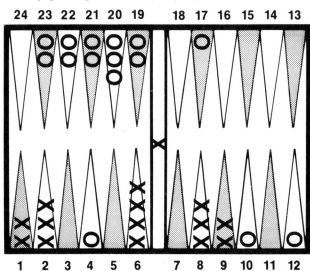

X moves bar/24, 6/3. The 1 enables him to re-enter, and he plays the 3 safely behind O.

Roll 11 for O
O to Play 4–2
(X 3–1 bar/24, 6/3)

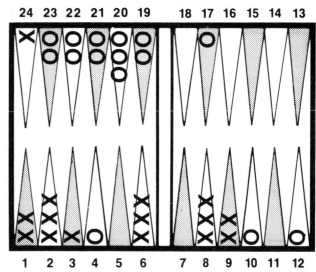

O moves 20/24*, 17/19. Here O takes a calculated risk in hitting X. It is true that X may re-enter with a 1 on the twenty-four point, sending O's blot all the way back to X's inner board. However, the odds are that X will not roll a 1, and O will then be able to close the sixth point in the inner board, completely shutting X out. This move also denies X the chance of rolling a 6, escaping from behind the prime and getting back into a winning race.

When examining the risks involved in being hit, you should not only consider the danger of losing ground in the race but also the danger of possibly failing to re-enter. In this case, X has only 3 points closed (O has 5), so O can be much more confident about re-entering should he be hit. Moving 17/19 brings another builder to bear directly on the twenty-four point; if X fails to re-enter, O can cover the point with a direct 5.

Since the nineteen point is closed, X fails to re-enter.

Roll 11 for X
X to Play 6–6
(O 4–2 20/24*, 17/19)

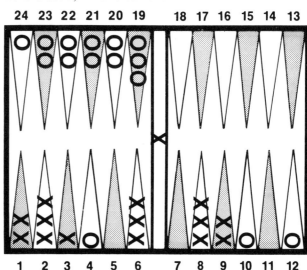

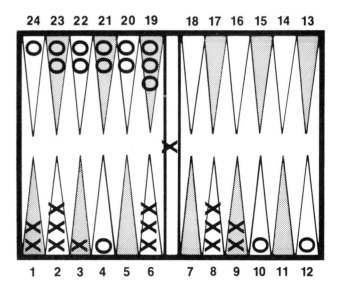

Roll 12 for O
O to Play 5–1
(X 6–6 O)

O moves 19/24, closing his board, and 4/5, bringing his last back man closer to freedom. At this point O continues rolling since there is no possible way for X to re-enter as long as all 6 inner-board points are closed. When O breaks one of these points, X may roll.

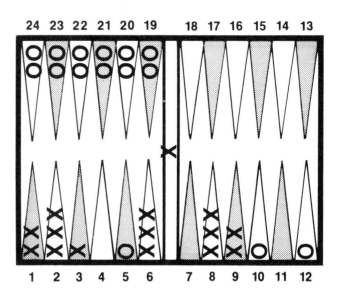

Roll 13 for O
O to Play 2–1
(O 5–1 19/24, 4/5)

O moves 5/7, 12/13 bringing his men closer to home.

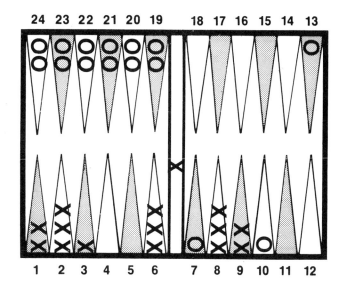

Roll 14 for O
O to Play 6–6
(O 2–1 5/7, 12/13)

O moves 7/19, 13/19, 10/16.

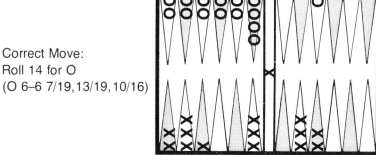

Correct Move:
Roll 14 for O
(O 6–6 7/19,13/19,10/16)

Let's stop for a moment to discuss the fundamental principles of bearing in and off *against opposition*, that is, when your opponent still has a man deep in your inner board or on the bar. In Game I we discussed the bear-off in a simple race, where the object was to bear off as *quickly* as possible; here we wish to bear off as *safely* as possible. Clearly, when your opponent is in a position to hit you, you do not bear a man off at every opportunity — especially if you must leave a blot to do so.

Here are some principles to follow:

1. Avoid leaving yourself vulnerable to "freak" doubles — doubles which force you to leave a shot. In the present position, if O rolls another 6–6, O will be forced to leave a shot after taking one man into his inner board and bearing three men off the nineteen point. There was nothing O could have done to avoid this on his previous roll. In many cases, however, a little extra precaution will keep your men safe from danger even if you roll high doubles.

Position A
X to Play 1

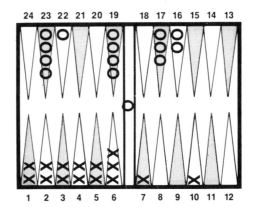

In Position A, for example, if X has a 1 to play he should not play 7/6 or 10/9, either of which will force him to leave a man exposed to 6–6 on the next roll. The correct play is 6/5. Now 6–6 and all other rolls play safely. 6–6 followed by being hit may seem like a remote possibility, but there is no reason to risk it since playing safely costs nothing.

2. When bearing into your inner board, avoid going in "deep"; in other words, to the one, two, or perhaps three point.

Position B

Position C

Position D

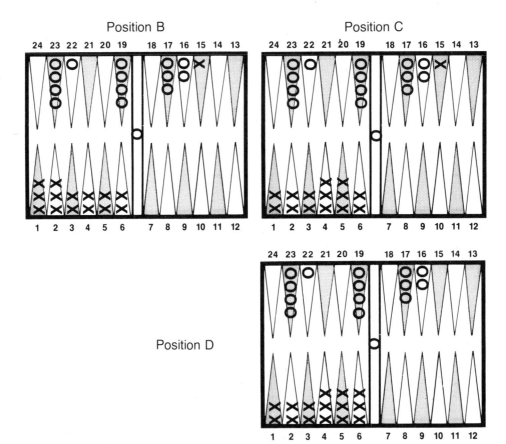

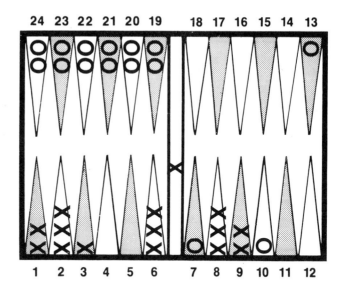

Roll 14 for O
O to Play 6–6
(O 2–1 5/7, 12/13)

O moves 7/19, 13/19, 10/16.

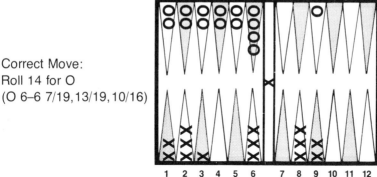

Correct Move:
Roll 14 for O
(O 6–6 7/19,13/19,10/16)

Let's stop for a moment to discuss the fundamental principles of bearing in and off *against opposition*, that is, when your opponent still has a man deep in your inner board or on the bar. In Game I we discussed the bear-off in a simple race, where the object was to bear off as *quickly* as possible; here we wish to bear off as *safely* as possible. Clearly, when your opponent is in a position to hit you, you do not bear a man off at every opportunity — especially if you must leave a blot to do so.

Here are some principles to follow:

1. Avoid leaving yourself vulnerable to "freak" doubles — doubles which force you to leave a shot. In the present position, if O rolls another 6–6, O will be forced to leave a shot after taking one man into his inner board and bearing three men off the nineteen point. There was nothing O could have done to avoid this on his previous roll. In many cases, however, a little extra precaution will keep your men safe from danger even if you roll high doubles.

Position A
X to Play 1

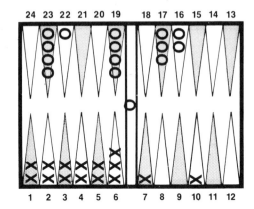

In Position A, for example, if X has a 1 to play he should not play 7/6 or 10/9, either of which will force him to leave a man exposed to 6–6 on the next roll. The correct play is 6/5. Now 6–6 and all other rolls play safely. 6–6 followed by being hit may seem like a remote possibility, but there is no reason to risk it since playing safely costs nothing.

2. When bearing into your inner board, avoid going in "deep"; in other words, to the one, two, or perhaps three point.

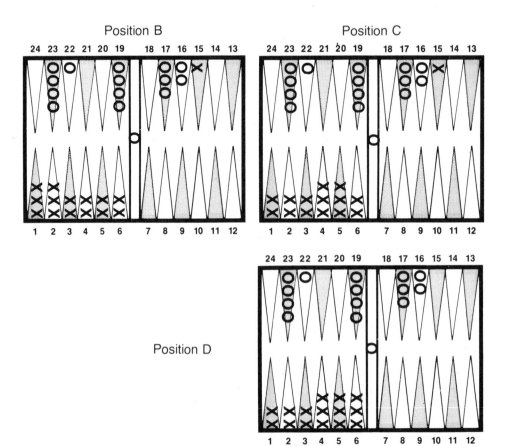

Position B

Position C

Position D

In Position B, X has brought two spare men deep to his one and two points. Although this position looks perfectly safe, it is much more dangerous than Position C, where X's two spare men are not deep.

By bringing men deep, you eliminate spare men. This hurts your flexibility and increases the chance for leaving a later shot. Position D is ideal, with spare men spread out on the high points.

3. When you bear off, clear your points in order beginning with points furthest from home. Don't leave gaps.

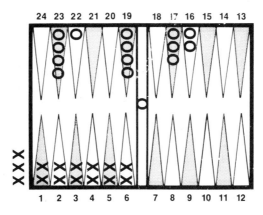

Position E
X to Play 5–3

In Position E the correct play is 6/1, 6/3.

4. Avoid leaving an isolated checker on your furthermost points. One way of doing this is to make sure that you have an *even* number of checkers on the highest points.

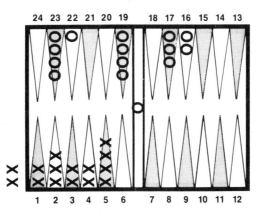

Position F
X to Play 5–2

In Position F you must not bear two men off 5/off, 2/off. This would leave a single spare checker on the five point and two high numbers on your next roll would force you to leave a shot.

The correct play is 5/off, 5/3. Remember that the object is to get off as safely as possible — not as quickly as possible.

Let's return now to the game.

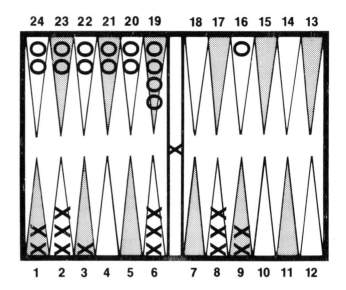

Roll 15 for O
O to Play 6–4
(O 6–6 7/19,
13/19, 10/16)

O moves 16/20, 19/off. This move allows him to safely play all future numbers and avoids going deep into his inner board. The alternate play 16/22, 19/23 would leave him with an isolated checker on the nineteen point.

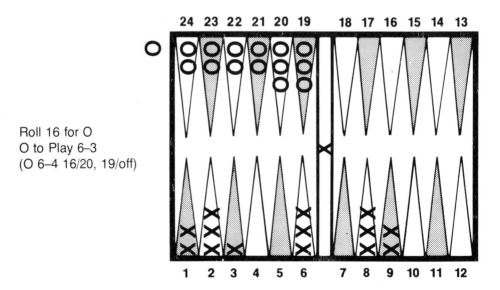

Roll 16 for O
O to Play 6–3
(O 6–4 16/20, 19/off)

O correctly moves 19/off, 20/23. Remember that just because you may legally bear two men off in this position you are not obligated to do so if you can take another legal move. If O moved 19/off, 22/off, he would leave a blot on the twenty-two point.

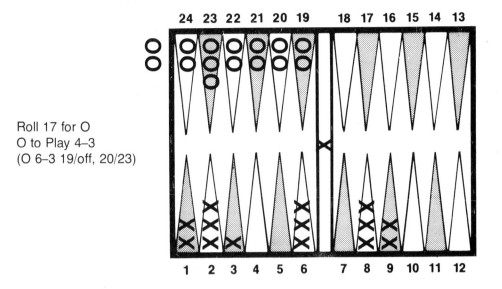

Roll 17 for O
O to Play 4–3
(O 6–3 19/off, 20/23)

O moves 19/23, 19/22. Again he wisely refrains from taking any men off and instead clears his points in order. He starts with the point furthest away from home — the nineteen point. Since this point is now open, X may finally take a roll.

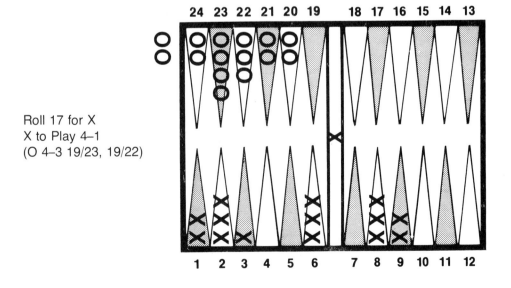

Roll 17 for X
X to Play 4–1
(O 4–3 19/23, 19/22)

X ∅. Unfortunately, both the twenty-one and twenty-four points are closed and X cannot re-enter.

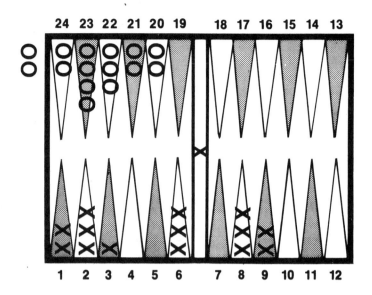

Roll 18 for O
O to Play 6–2
(X 4–1 Ø)

O moves 20/off, 20/22. This roll leaves him in an extremely safe position since he has an even number of checkers on the points furthest from home.

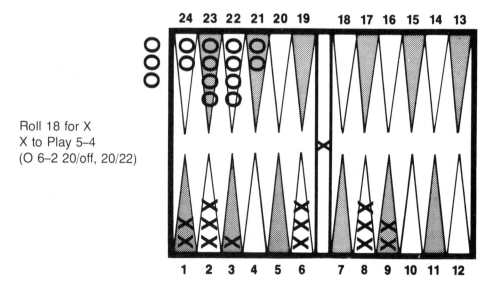

Roll 18 for X
X to Play 5–4
(O 6–2 20/off, 20/22)

X moves bar/16, successfully re-entering on the twenty point with the 5 and moving on to the sixteen point with the 4 in the race to get home.

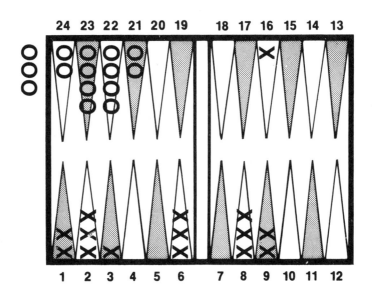

Roll 19 for O
O to Play 2–2
(X 5–4 bar/16)

O moves 23/off(4). Since the last opposing man has come in and is on the way home, O can begin bearing off expeditiously. This technique — bearing off without opposition — was described in Game I. O wants to bear off as many men as possible on each roll.

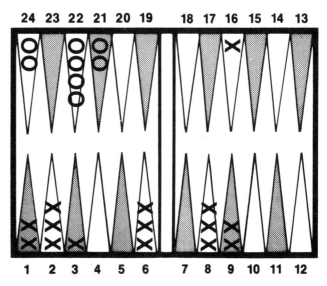

Roll 19 for X
X to Play 4–3
(O 2–2 23/off [4])

X moves 16/12, 9/6. X is clearly hopelessly behind in the race and has no chance to win. The game continues, however, to see whether or not X will lose a **gammon,** or double game. A gammon, you remember, occurs when a player bears off all his men before his opponent bears off any.

X cannot begin his bear-off until *all* his men are in his inner board. In order to avoid being gammoned, he must get his men home as quickly and as efficiently as possible. X should therefore use all his pips economically, taking them outside his home board and avoiding wasting them in his home board. He is trying to basically pile all his men up on his six point. If X played his 4 by moving 9/5 (or worse yet, 8/4), he would be using a pip or two inside his inner board that should be used outside.

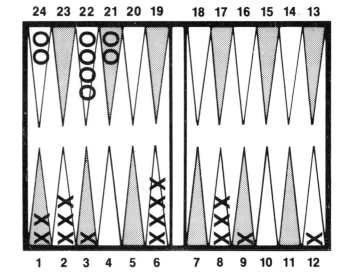

Roll 20 for O
O to Play 3–1
(X 4–3 16/12, 9/6)

O moves 22/off, 24/off.

Roll 20 for X
X to Play 5–2
(O 3–1 22/off, 24/off)

X moves 12/7, 8/6.

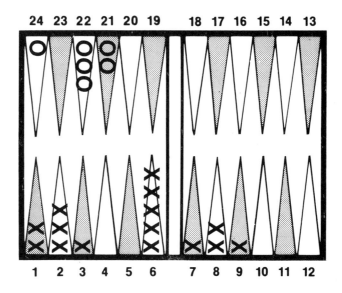

Roll 21 for O
O to Play 5–3
(X 5–2 12/7, 8/6)

O moves 21/off, 22/off.

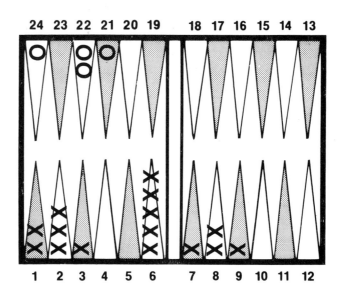

Roll 21 for X
X to Play 6–3
(O 5–3 21/off, 22/off)

X moves 9/3, 8/5. The race to save the gammon promises to be close.

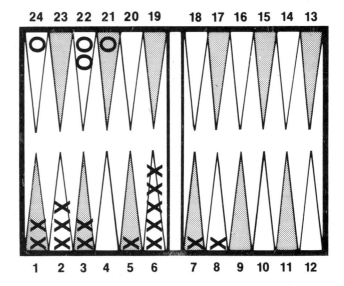

Roll 22 for O
O to Play 3–1
(X 6–3 9/3, 8/5)

O moves 22/off, 24/off.

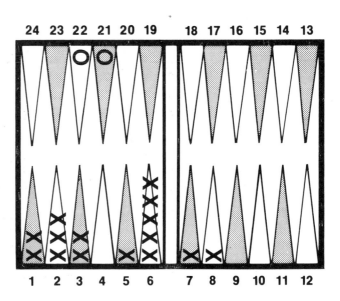

Roll 22 for X
X to Play 2–1
(O 3–1 22/off, 24/off)

X moves 7/4. This is a strategic play that may save X the gammon. By making the "normal" play of bringing both men in (8/6, 7/6 as seen below), X looks as if he is guaranteed to get a man off next roll, but a closer inspection reveals that 4–4 fails to take any men off.

By moving correctly 7/4, X will be able to remove a man on his next turn no matter what he rolls. That is, if he is given the opportunity to roll. O may be able to bear his two remaining men off immediately (the chances are almost even).

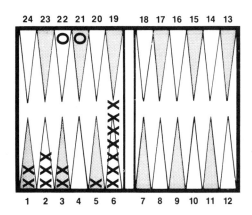

Alternate Move:
Roll 22 for X
(X 2–1 8/6, 7/6)

Roll 23 for O
O to Play 2–2
(X 2–1 7/4)

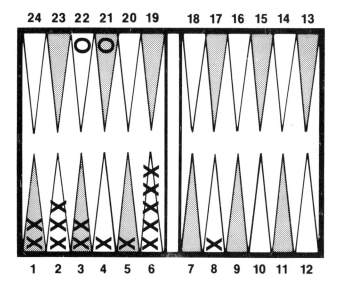

O moves 21/off, 22/off, winning the game and gammoning X!

Summary for Game II and Opening Moves

1. The best points on your side to own are, in order of importance, your five point, bar point, and four point. (When given the choice of making the bar point or five point, the five point is usually preferable.)

Although inner-board points are a threat to your opponent, it is usually not advisable to make the deep points (one, two, and sometimes three) too early in the game.

Points have more blocking value if they are made together, avoiding large gaps.

2. In order to make points quickly, it is essential to create builders to bear on the points you wish to make. Small risks (such as a few indirect shots) may be necessary to create builders.

3. It is of great value to establish an **advanced anchor** (your opponent's four or five point). Such a point is more important than any point you can make on your side of the board.

Beginners often make their opponent's two point. Although this gives you an anchor on which to re-enter, it is more difficult to escape from than the one point. Many games are lost by making the two point and never being able to leave it.

4. If your opponent has a point in your inner board, the single most effective blocking point is the one 6 pips in front of him. (This is another reason why it is wrong to make your opponent's two point. Since your opponent begins the game holding the eight point, you place yourself directly in front of the point that most effectively blocks you.)

5. Your midpoint has strategic value whenever you have men in your opponent's inner board, or on his bar point. If you are behind in the race, the midpoint may aid your holding game by making it harder for your opponent to extricate his back men and clear *his* midpoint. If you want to escape your own back men, the midpoint usually serves as the only safe landing space in the outer boards.

6. When bearing off against opposition (that is, when your opponent holds a deep point in your inner board, or is on the bar), you want to bear off as *safely* as possible. There are four principles to follow:

A. Avoid bringing your spare checkers *deep* into your inner board. Leave them spread out on points further from home.

B. Begin by clearing your points in order, starting from the point furthest from home. By doing this you can avoid leaving gaps.

C. Avoid situations where two high numbers will force you to leave a blot. Do not leave a single spare checker on your furthermost points. This can be done by leaving an even number of checkers on the furthermost points.

D. Plan ahead, if possible, so that large doubles (usually 5–5 or 6–6) will play safely.

7. There are two basic cases when you bear in without opposition: when you want to save the gammon, or when the game is a simple race.

A. Saving the gammon is the simplest case of bearing in because you try to bring your men in as quickly and efficiently as possible. You should not waste any pips in your inner board, but move them all in the outer boards. (Exception: Sometimes when only one roll remains, moving a pip in the inner board gives you a better chance to bear off on the next roll.)

B. In a race, although you are trying to bring your men in as quickly as possible in order to bear off, it is unwise to pile them all up on the six point. It is better to "waste" a few pips when bearing in in order to make sure that the four and five points have enough spare checkers. In this way, even if you lose a roll bearing your first man off, you will usually get your last man off quicker.

C. When bearing in, with or without opposition, you should try to maximize the number of **cross-overs.** A cross-over means moving a checker from one quadrant to another. Do this as efficiently as possible, moving 1 or 2 pips into the next quadrant, not 5 or 6.

CHAPTER 7.
BASIC DOUBLING
STRATEGY

DOUBLING IS ONE of the most important and exacting aspects of backgammon. Good doubling decisions will often make the difference between winning and losing a series of games.

Let us review the rules:

The doubling cube starts out "in the middle." That is, either player may double whenever he feels he has a significant advantage. In doubling, he offers to double the stakes of the game by turning the cube to 2 and passing it to his opponent. The double must be made when the player is on roll, but *before* he has rolled the dice.

His opponent then has two options:

1. He may refuse (**pass**) the double and lose the original one unit, thus ending the game.

2. He may accept (**take**) the double, in which case the game continues with a value of two units — double the original stake.

The player who has been doubled is said to **own the cube,** which gives him the exclusive right to re-double should he feel at any time that *he* is the favorite. If he re-doubles, his opponent may pass, giving up the present stake of the game — two units; or he can take, playing on at the re-doubled stake of four units.

Re-doubling can, in theory, continue on forever, keeping in mind that only the player who owns the cube (the last player to have been doubled) may offer a re-double. Experienced players seldom re-double a game beyond the four or eight level.

Offering Doubles

The question of when you possess a sufficient advantage to warrant doubling is unanswerable in easy terms. The player owning the cube has a built-in advantage in that he alone may decide whether to make the next double. You should therefore avoid doubling with a trifling advantage, for this gives your opponent ownership of the cube (which can be a powerful weapon against you) too cheaply. On the other hand, you must have the courage to double when you have a solid lead.

The double may have two effects: First, it may force your opponent to pass, thus ensuring a definite win. Failure to double allows your opponent to play on "for free" and possibly get a lucky sequence of rolls to reverse the position and win the game. In such a case you have only yourself, not the dice, to blame.

Secondly, if your opponent takes, he is now faced with a loss of twice as much. Failure to double allows him to escape with a lesser penalty than he deserves. In backgammon there is no reward for such humane treatment — your opponent cannot be expected to extend the same courtesy to you.

Taking Doubles

Assume that you have been doubled. Unless your opponent has made a serious miscalculation, he is the favorite. Why, then, should you consider taking at all and playing on at a higher stake?

The answer is that by passing you give up a sure point, whereas by taking you may hope to turn the tide of the game and win two points yourself. Thus, if you have a reasonable chance to win, you are better off taking than resigning yourself to a sure loss.

What constitutes reasonable? One criterion often used is whether you have better than a 25% chance to win the game. However, except in a few well-defined endgame situations, there is no practical way of evaluating what the true odds of winning actually are.

Every position is different, so there is no easy formula for deciding what your practical chances are in a given position. In fact, many of the world's best players often disagree strongly about the merits of accepting certain doubles.

Gammon Possibilities

Sometimes your position will rapidly become so overwhelmingly strong that you have virtually no chance of losing and have an excellent chance of gammoning your opponent. In such a case, doubling would be a great error — because your game is *too* good. If you double, your opponent will quickly pass, giving you half what you would gain if you played the game out and gammoned him.

Gammon possibilities may also strongly influence your decision about whether to *accept* a double. Consider the case where you have a reasonable chance to win, but sense that you will be gammoned if you lose. In such a case, you must be far more careful in accepting, for you are risking losing not twice as much, but four times as much. (This is one reason why the 25% rule mentioned earlier for taking doubles is not always an adequate criterion.)

Conversely, when considering whether to double, if you have a significant chance to gammon your opponent but run little risk of being gammoned yourself, you may consider doubling earlier than usual. The ability to judge when a position involves a possible gammon comes with experience.

In sum, good doubling strategy goes hand in hand with a knowledge of the game — the ability to correctly assess positions and predict the game's resolution. As you play more and read further in this book, you will acquire an understanding of the underlying concepts of the game, which in turn will better enable you to assess your overall chances.

Note: The question of when to double and when to take in a racing position is discussed in Chapter 10.

CHAPTER 8.
GAME III: PRIMING GAME

BACKGAMMON IS NOT just a game of running and hitting, but also very much a game of position. Game III illustrates the importance of blocking your opponent's back men.

The best way to block your opponent is to form several points in a row. Such a sequence of consecutive points is called a **prime.** Game III illustrates how blockading or priming your opponent can be an effective winning strategy. In particular, we emphasize the strength of a 6-point or full prime (6 points together in sequence).

As we saw in Game II, the player who takes an early lead in the race is not necessarily the winner. In fact, his lead may prove ultimately to be his undoing! For this reason, Game III also illustrates the strategic concept of *timing.* As you become more experienced, you will learn to evaluate not only the immediate position, but also the game's long-range evolution.

In Game III we introduce the doubling cube. You should begin playing with the cube in practice games. At first you may be unsure about when to double or take; however, as you gain experience and are better able to evaluate positions, you will gradually obtain a better understanding of when you possess a sufficient advantage to double, and, if doubled, whether you should accept or refuse the cube.

In the diagrams, the doubling cube is shown at first in the middle. This means that either player may, before he rolls the dice, offer the first double.

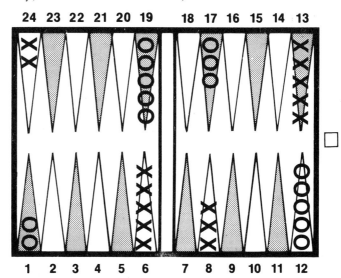

Roll 1
X 3, O 2, X to Play 3–2

X has won the first roll. The correct play is 13/10, 13/11, bringing two builders down from his midpoint.

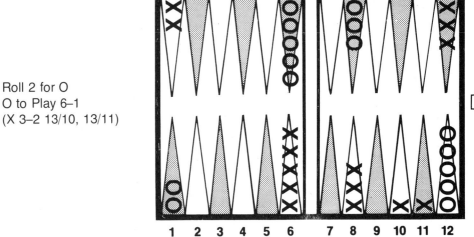

Roll 2 for O
O to Play 6–1
(X 3–2 13/10, 13/11)

O moves 12/18, 17/18, making his bar point.

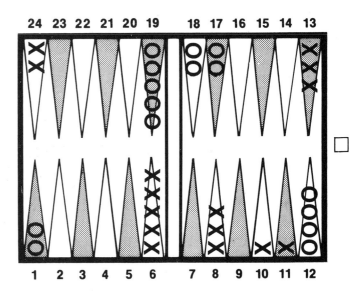

Roll 2 for X
X to Play 5–1
(O 6–1 12/18, 17/18)

X moves 10/5, 6/5, making the five point. The five point is X's most valuable point on his side of the board. It is generally more valuable than the bar point. If X had rolled 6–1, with a choice of making either the five or bar point, the correct move would be to make the five point.

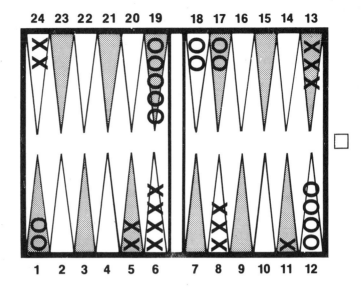

Roll 3 for O
O to Play 5–3
(X 5–1 10/5, 6/5)

O moves 12/17, 12/15, bringing two builders down to bear upon the twenty and twenty-one points (or O's four and five points). This move is preferable to making the twenty-two point (O's three point).

The alternate move 1/9 is too risky since this man would be exposed to a double shot.

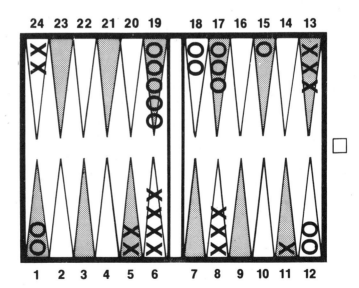

Roll 3 for X
X to Play 6–4
(O 5–3 12/17, 12/15)

This is another good roll. X moves 13/7, 11/7, making a point. Now X has four points in a row and is well on his way to effectively blocking and trapping O's back men.

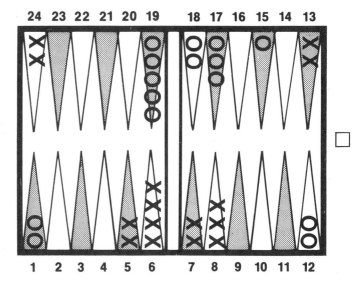

Roll 4 for O
O to Play 6–5
(X 6–4 13/7, 11/7)

O moves 12/18, 12/17. Ordinarily, on an opening roll, O would be able to move one of his back runners to safety on his midpoint 1/12, but X's blockade prevents this. The indicated play is the only way to move without exposing himself to a direct shot.

Backgammon is a game of position where big numbers in themselves are often not favorable. Here, O is forced to relinquish his midpoint, the twelve point. As a general principle, one should try to maintain this point — especially if there are still men trapped back in the opposing inner board. By giving up this point, the back runners become stranded from the other checkers and have no safe landing place in the **outfield** (both outer boards).

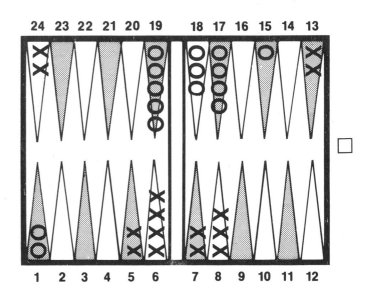

Roll 4 for X
X to Play 4–2
(O 6–5 12/18, 12/17)

X moves 8/4, 6/4, making the four point and constructing a 5-point prime.

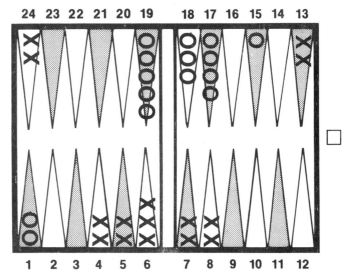

Roll 5 for O
O to Play 4–4
(X 4–2 8/4, 6/4)

O moves 17/21(2), 19/23(2), making 2 points in his inner board. The two point is not very desirable but is the best available. Once again, the value of large numbers per se is misleading; O must extricate his two back runners before racing numbers have any value.

X *doubles; O accepts the double.* While both X and O have the same number of points, X has a far superior position because he has 5 points together to form a solid prime. For reasons that will be clear in two or three moves, X has reason to believe that O's position will deteriorate.

The fact that X has doubled will be indicated on the diagrams by the cube's position on O's side of the board. After this initial double, O alone has the option of re-doubling.

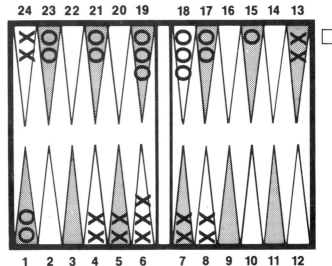

Roll 5 for X
X to Play 5–3
(O 4–4 17/21 [2],
    19/23 [2])

X moves 6/3, 8/3 maintaining the 5-point prime while advancing further into his inner board. This further restricts O and also threatens to allow X to achieve a full 6-point prime by rolling a 5. The opportunity to construct a full prime is well worth the risk of being hit by a specific 6–1 (a 17-to-1 shot).

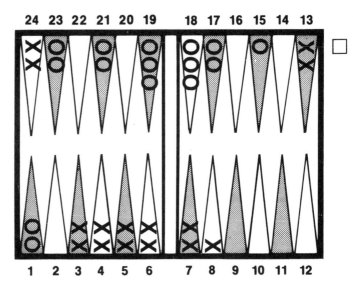

Roll 6 for O
O to Play 5–2
(X 5–3 6/3, 8/3)

O moves 15/20, 18/20. This is an excellent roll giving O a 5-point prime.

Let us stop now and assess the position. Both sides have 5-point primes, so superficially the positions seem similar. Both X and O have back men seemingly trapped. Does this mean that the game will be a stand-off with neither player able to escape?

No! Both players must keep moving forward whether they like it or not until eventually their primes collapse. Who, then, will be able to maintain his prime longest?

The answer is that X will since he has two spare men on his midpoint to play with, whereas O is rapidly running out of moves. The men on X's midpoint give him *time* (timing often is the crucial factor in advanced play).

As you become more sophisticated in backgammon, you will learn to view

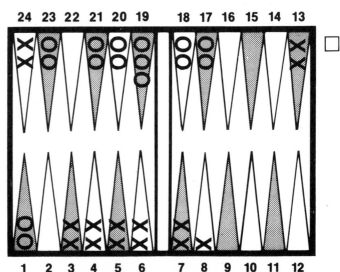

Roll 6 for X
X to Play 4–1
(O 5–2 15/20, 18/20)

each position not as a static entity but part of a pattern that continually changes. When X doubled, he anticipated that time was on his side. O is ahead if the position is viewed as a race. However, it is precisely because O is ahead in the race that he has less time to maintain his prime. In such a position, *large* numbers on the dice are disadvantageous.

X moves 13/8 forming a full 6-point prime. Forming a 6-point prime is always your ultimate objective when trying to trap your opponent. As long as the prime remains intact, there is no possible way for O to bypass it, regardless of what he rolls. The only way to ever get past a 6-point prime is to wait until your opponent breaks it up.

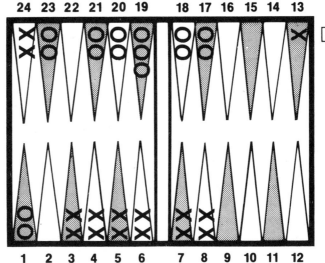

Roll 7 for O
O to Play 4–3
(X 4–1 13/8)

O moves 17/21, 17/20. The disintegration of his prime begins. O would, of course, rather not move at all, but the rules require every move to be played if legally possible.

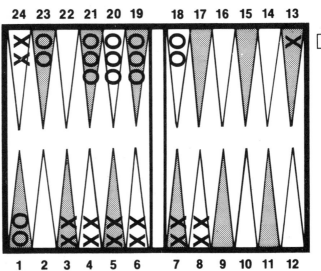

Roll 7 for X
X to Play 4–2
(O 4–3 17/21, 17/20)

X moves 13/9, 24/22. At first glance, this move may appear extremely reckless. O has countless ways to point on X's two blots. Why, then, does X take this chance?

The answer is that X has a full 6-point prime. X does not care whether he is pointed on or not. O can never escape his back runners, so he must continue moving his remaining men, even if it leads to his own self-destruction.

Roll 8 for O
O to Play 6–3
(X 4–2 24/22, 13/9)

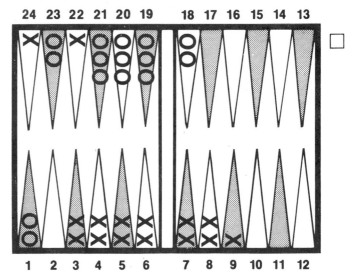

O moves 18/24*, 21/24 pointing on X.

Roll 8 for X
X to Play 5–2
(O 6–3 18/24*, 21/24)

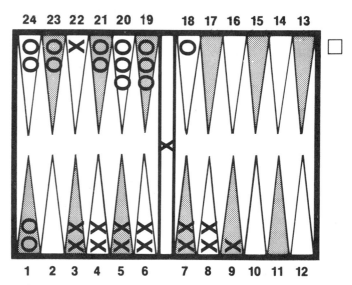

X ø; X fails to re-enter.

On Roll 9, O moves 18/22*, 20/22, pointing on a second blot. At this time, O has completely closed X out with two men on the bar. Ordinarily, closing one's opponent out allows for an almost certain win, as in Game II. Here, however, the close-out merely underscores the strength of X's 6-point prime and the futility of O's position.

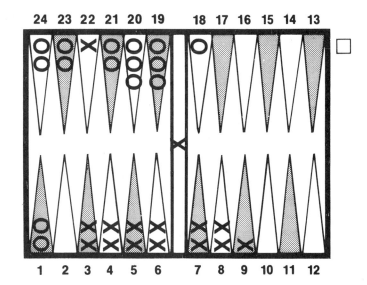

Roll 9 for O
O to Play 4–2
(X 5–2 Ø)

If you examine the position carefully, you will see that no conceivable set of rolls will allow O to escape his back runners. Since X is closed out, he cannot play and need not even bother rolling the dice. No matter what O rolls in the meantime, he will eventually be forced to open points in his inner board and allow X to come in. Remember that the rules do not allow O to bear any men off until *all* his men are in his own inner board.

O continues to roll.

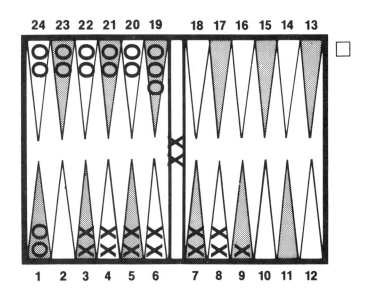

Roll 10 for O
O to Play 5–1
(O 4–2 18/22*, 20/22)

O moves 19/24, 1/2. O realizes his position is lost and begins to clear the point furthest from home first to avoid possibly exposing a man in his inner board. Allowing a third man to be sent back would increase the chance that he would be gammoned.

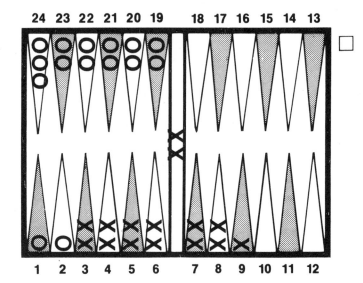

Roll 11 for O
O to Play 4–3
(O 5–1 19/24, 1/2)

O moves 19/22, 19/23. He is forced to break a point in his inner board. This solution is one that is commonly misplayed. When establishing points in the inner board, you try to make the points furthest away from home first. Nevertheless, when you are forced to break up your board, it is important to give up the points *in order* starting with those *furthest* away from home. In this position, O has the choice of clearing either the nineteen or twenty point; he correctly chooses to clear the nineteen point first.

X can now roll.

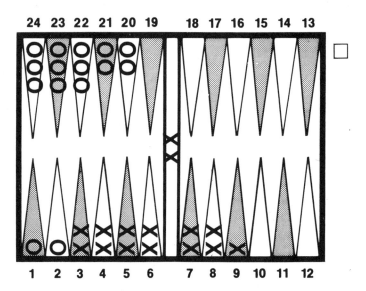

Roll 11 for X
X to Play 6–1
(O 4–3 19/22, 19/23)

X moves bar/19, ø. He is forced to bring a man in on the nineteen point with the 6. X is unable to re-enter the second man with the 1, and he cannot legally take the 1 elsewhere.

Roll 12 for O
O to Play 6–4
(X 6–1 bar/19, Ø)

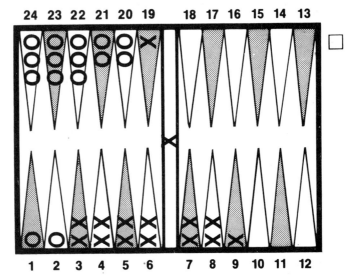

O moves 20/24, ø. The 4 is forced; there is no legal 6.

Roll 12 for X
X to Play 6–3
(O 6–4 20/24, Ø)

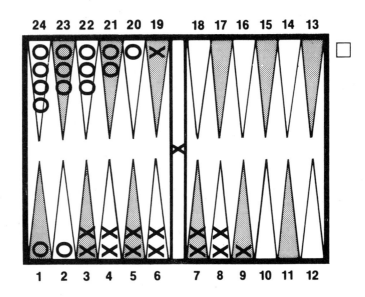

X moves bar/19, 9/6. X had hoped to roll a 5 hitting O's blot. X moves 9/6 to bring his spare checker into range to attack O's back runners.

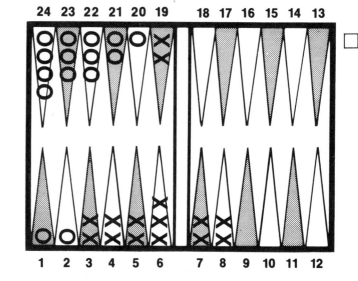

Roll 13 for O
O to Play 4–1
(X 6–3 bar/19, 9/6)

O moves 20/24, 1/2. Although he has little chance of winning the game, it is imperative that he bring his back men together for safety. If O leaves his back men exposed, he may be closed out — this would give X a definite chance to win a gammon. By maintaining the two point, O should avoid being gammoned.

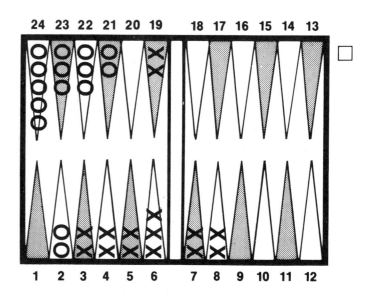

Roll 13 for X
X to Play 6–6
(O 4–1 1/2, 20/24)

X moves 19/7(2). These big doubles are not really advantageous since X is free to move his men around the board at his leisure. X's play is certainly sound and should lead to an easy win.

The more experienced and/or greedy player may wish to experiment with another play: 19/13(2), 7/1(2)!

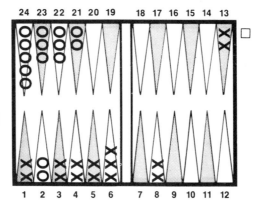

Alternate Move:
Roll 13 for X
(X 6–6 19/13 [2], 7/1 [2])

This trap play may appear foolish since X breaks his prime before he has to and gives O the chance to escape with a 5. Actually, X is setting a cunning trap: He *hopes* that O will come out with one 5. (Note that if O rolled one 5 he would have no choice but to emerge from the two point since he has no legal 5's elsewhere.)

Since O has destroyed part of his board, and since X now has a 5-point board, X hopes to lure O out and then pounce on his two defenseless blots. If X succeeds in picking up the two blots and closing O out, X will have greatly enhanced his chance for winning a gammon (four points, since the game has been doubled once).

Of course, this alternate strategy is not without some risk. O might come out with 5–5 and win the resulting race easily, or X might have trouble hitting and closing O out after a single 5. In either case, X may be jeopardizing a potentially won game for the added chance for a gammon. The expert would evaluate the net gain as worth the risk, but we shall pursue the game along the safer indicated path.

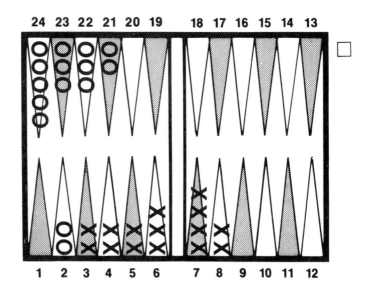

Roll 14 for O
O to Play 6–3
(X 6–6 19/7 [2])

O moves 21/24, ø.

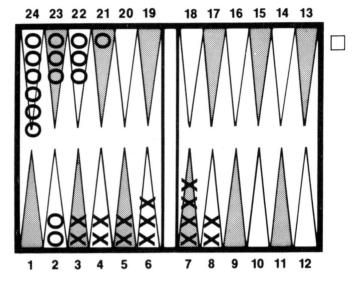

Roll 14 for X
X to Play 5–4
(O 6–3 21/24, Ø)

X moves 8/3, 8/4. X wishes to come home safely. The principles for bearing in safely when your opponent holds a point in your inner board are basically the same as those in bearing off:

1. Clear your points in order from the point furthest away from home, hoping to avoid leaving gaps.

2. Avoid, if possible, bearing your extra men in deep.

3. Avoid, if possible, bearing a single spare checker in on the point furthest away from home.

An alternate move would be 6/1, 7/3, which would maintain X's full prime one additional roll.

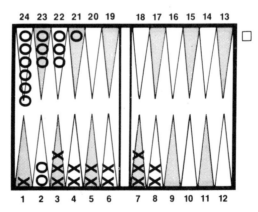

Alternate Move:
Roll 14 for X
(X 5–4 6/1, 7/3)

This move would leave a potentially dangerous position. Putting spare checkers deep on the three point and leaving a spare checker on the seven point is a possible source of trouble; 6–1, 6–3, 6–4, and 6–5, for example, would all force you to leave an exposed man. Even at this late stage in the game, care must be taken to bear in correctly and avoid accidents.

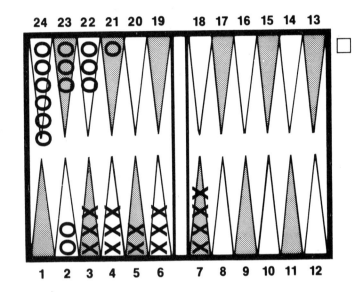

Roll 15 for O
O to Play 5–2
(X 5–4 8/3, 8/4)

O moves 21/23, ø.

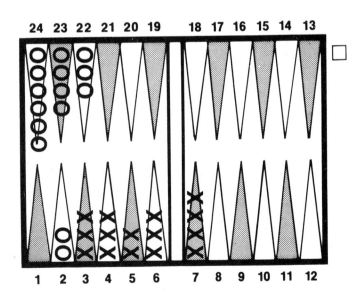

Roll 15 for X
X to Play 6–4
(O 5–2 21/23, Ø)

X moves 7/1, 7/3.

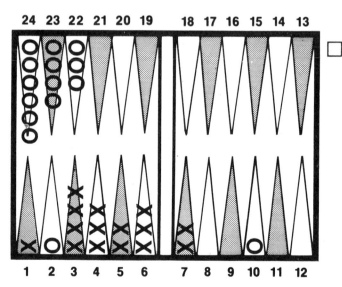

Roll 16 for O
O to Play 6–2
(X 6–4 7/1, 7/3)

O moves one checker 2/10, escaping from behind X's prime. Even if O escapes his second back man, he will find he has fallen far behind in the race.

Roll 16 for X
X to Play 2–1
(O 6–2 2/10)

X moves 4/2*, 3/2. This is another play where care must be exercised. Let's look at the alternate moves.

First, X could have played 7/5, 7/6, as seen in Alternate Move #1.

This move, in preparation for bearing off, would give X a substantial lead (although a lucky 6–6 for O would bring O far ahead).

A second alternate move would be 4/2*/1, hitting and covering the one point without leaving a blot.

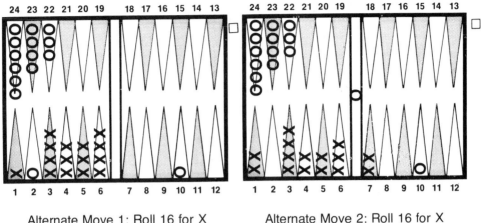

Alternate Move 1: Roll 16 for X
(X 2–1 7/5, 7/6)

Alternate Move 2: Roll 16 for X
(X 2–1 4/2*/1)

Playing 4/2*, 3/2 is recommended above these two alternatives. It gives O the least chance for a lucky win despite the blot on the one point. X has again reconstructed a full 6-point prime (from the two point through the seven point) and therefore need not fear being hit on the one point.

The key idea here is that even if O re-enters on the one point, his man can never escape and so X is in no danger. In fact, it is probably to X's advantage to have O re-enter on the one point so that X has a chance to come around again and possibly hit the blot now on the ten point. Such a series of events would give X good gammon prospects.

Roll 17 for O
O to Play 5–5
(X 2–1 4/2*, 3/2)

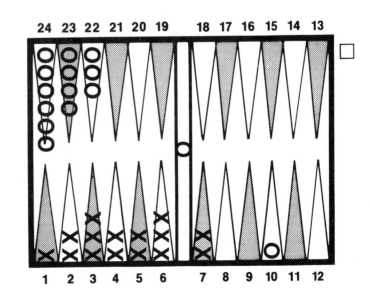

O ø.

Roll 17 for X
X to Play 6–2
(O 5–5 Ø)

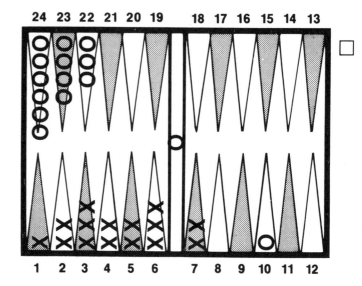

X moves 7/1, 7/5. O is closed out, and X continues to roll.

Roll 18 for X
X to Play 6–1
(X 6–2 7/1, 7/5)

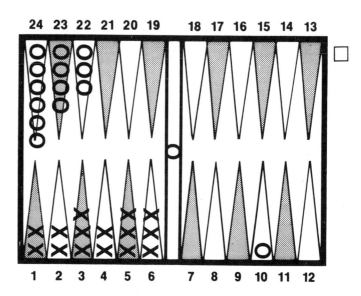

X moves 6/off, 5/4. Remember that when you bear off against opposition (opposition here being the O blot lurking on the bar), you do not remove your men as quickly as possible, but as safely as possible. X's play leaves him in a position where no roll can force him to leave a shot.

If X had carelessly played 6/off, 3/2, he would be left with a spare checker near the right-hand side of his board.

This move could potentially lead to trouble; a subsequent 5–5 or 6–6 would leave a shot.

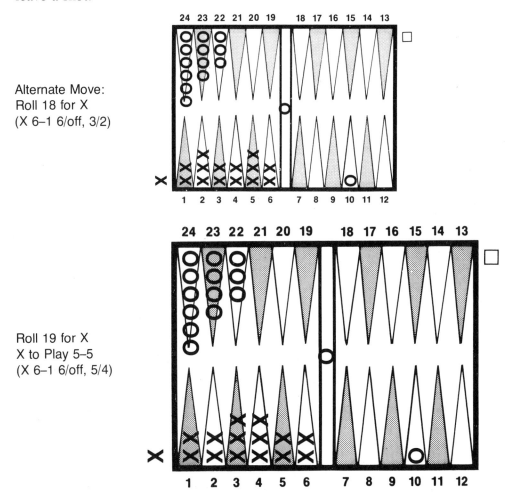

Alternate Move:
Roll 18 for X
(X 6–1 6/off, 3/2)

Roll 19 for X
X to Play 5–5
(X 6–1 6/off, 5/4)

X moves 6/1(2), 5/off(2). Because he played his last move with care, X is able to safely play 5–5. Little sympathy should be extended to a player who played the alternate move on Roll 18 and was subsequently hit after leaving a blot on Roll 19. Such a player might bemoan his fate and declare how unlucky he is, but we can see that his pitfall can be prevented at no cost.

Occasionally, even with the best bear-off technique, you will lose a game because of an unfortunate sequence of rolls which forces you to leave a shot which is hit. It is, in fact, the potential for disaster in seemingly won positions that makes backgammon exciting. If you follow the rules for bearing off, however, you will have fewer tales of woe to tell.

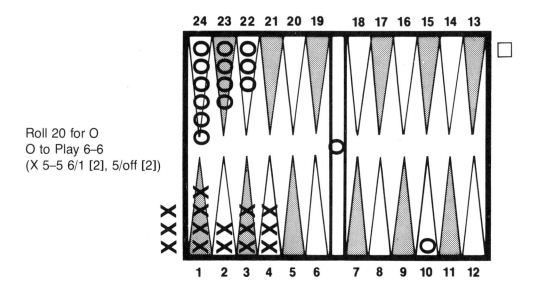

Roll 20 for O
O to Play 6–6
(X 5–5 6/1 [2], 5/off [2])

O moves bar/18, 10/16. With this roll, any chance of O's being gammoned is eliminated. We leave the game now since the rest is a simple bear-off, which X should be able to win quite easily. Since X doubled the game earlier, X should win two points.

Game III Summary

1. One of the basic objectives in backgammon is to block your opponent's forward progress and especially to trap his back men. This is usually done by forming points in a row, called a **prime**. The more points you own in a row, the more difficult it becomes for your opponent to bypass the blockade. A 5-point prime is extremely difficult to bypass, especially if your opponent is not directly in front of it (at the edge of the prime). Ideally, you wish to form a 6-point prime, a full prime. This is then impossible to bypass — any checker trapped behind a full prime must wait until the player possessing the prime dissolves it himself.

The value of the full prime is underscored by the fact that the player owning it can afford to have some of his remaining men hit, and even closed out, without jeopardizing his game. (If you are unsure of the reason for this, review Game III to understand this important idea.)

2. Often the only way to defeat a prime which you are trapped behind is to form your own prime to trap your opponent. The idea is to force him to break *his* prime first.

3. When you have closed your inner board but are unfortunately forced to break it up, it is best to break the points furthest away from home first.

4. When you have a commanding lead in the race and wish merely to come home safely, care must still be taken to bear in and off safely. You must exercise vigilance even in "won" positions to avoid unpleasant "accidents."

The principles for successful bearing in are basically the same as for bearing off:

      A. Clear your points in order beginning with the point furthest away from home in order to avoid leaving gaps.

      B. Avoid, if possible, bearing your extra men in deep.

      C. Avoid, if possible, leaving an isolated spare man on your point furthest away from home. Try to leave an even number of men there.

  5. Even when the game is hopeless, take care not to compound the loss by being needlessly gammoned. Conversely, even in positions where you are an almost certain winner, you should examine ways to increase your win with a gammon.

CHAPTER 9.
GAME IV:
ATTACKING GAME

THE FINAL SAMPLE game demonstrates another winning game plan: the **attack.** Some games of backgammon are long, protracted positional struggles, while others — such as this one — may be decided quickly by a series of sharp blows.

After finishing this game, you should review the basic winning methods in all four games (running, holding, priming, and attacking). It is never correct strategy to have one preconceived game plan; rather, you must be flexible and choose the best one as the position evolves. Familiarity with all four of these basic strategies will come with experience.

This game illustrates special advanced tactical plays which demonstrate that even in seemingly routine positions you must be careful to make the best play.

Roll 1
O 5, X 2, O to Play 5–2

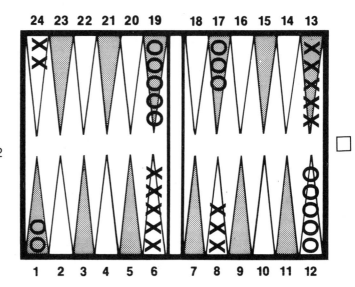

O moves 12/17, 12/14.

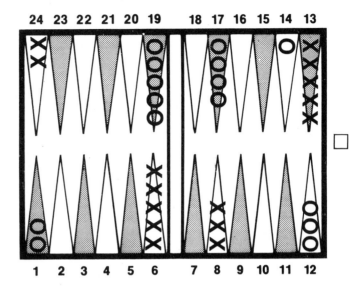

Roll 2 for X
X to Play 4–4
(O 5–2 12/17, 12/14)

X moves 24/20(2), 13/9(2). 4–4 allows you to make what is considered to be the strongest opening move: establishing your opponent's five point (the twenty point here). This is the single most important point for you to control in the middle game.

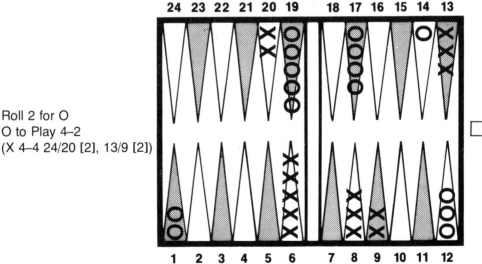

Roll 2 for O
O to Play 4–2
(X 4–4 24/20 [2], 13/9 [2])

O moves 1/5, 12/14. When your opponent holds a point in your inner board, the most effective blocking point is the one which is 6 pips in front of him (5 pips in front is also excellent). Since X has succeeded in making the twenty point, O rightly makes the fourteen point 12/14. Similarly, if X had made the twenty-two point, O would then make the sixteen point to block effectively.

Since X has made the valuable twenty point, O would like to equalize the position by making the five point. O therefore splits to the five point, 1/5, hoping to cover it on a subsequent roll. It is usually risky to come up to your opponent's four or five point when he has extra builders bearing on these points.

Roll 3 for X
X to Play 3–1
(O 4–2 12/14, 1/5)

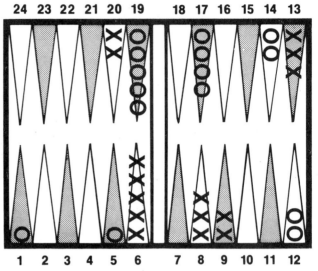

X moves 8/5*, 6/5. This excellent roll makes the important five point and also hits O's blot. X now controls both his five point and O's five point, and X has the beginnings of a good blocking position since he controls the five, six, eight, and nine points.

Roll 3 for O
O to Play 4–2
(X 3–1 8/5*, 6/5)

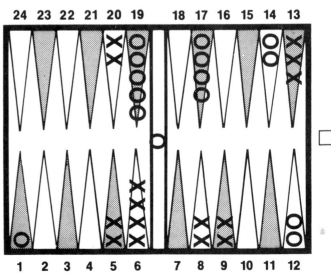

O moves bar/4, 19/21. Again O chooses the somewhat more dangerous line of play by re-entering on the four point rather than the two point. O realizes that the game has not been going very well for him, and his move bar/4 is a gamble to improve his standing. He hopes to make the four point on a subsequent roll and establish an advanced anchor in X's board.

O simultaneously slots a man on the twenty-one point 19/21. He wants to build up his inner board quickly in order to threaten X.

X, however, has no intention of letting O equalize the game. He decides to take advantage of his present superiority.

X *doubles!* This double demonstrates the tremendous variability of the game. Many games last a large number of moves — even going as far as the end of the bear-off — before one player possesses a sufficient advantage to double; in other games, as here, one side is able to double after only three moves.

O *accepts.* Although it is certainly understandable that O is reluctant to decline the double (and lose one point) in a game only three moves old, an experienced player would see that the position is very dangerous. O is exposed to a powerful attack and, if the attack is successful, will probably be gammoned. By accepting the double, then, O ultimately risks losing not one extra point, but three since if he is gammoned he will lose four points.

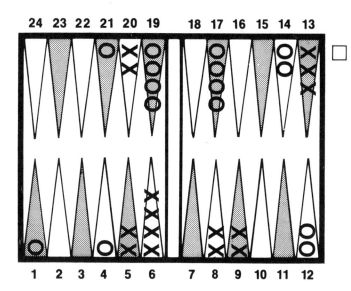

Roll 4 for X
X to Play 3–2
(O 4–2 bar/4, 19/21)

X moves 6/4*/1*. X launches his attack! Ordinarily, X would be reluctant to hit in his inner board with a blot since he would lose ground in the race by being hit back. Here, however (as in most cases in advanced play), the loss or gain of pips is not the most important consideration.

X can afford to be hit back since he has a secure anchor on the twenty point. Holding this **golden point** gives him enormous security, so much so that even after a most unfavorable sequence of rolls, X is almost certain to have a playable and probably still favorable game.

The reason for X's double early in the game (and why O should have passed) is becoming increasingly clear. If X is successful with his attack, he stands to gammon O. And even if X's attack is not an immediate success, merely owning the golden point assures X of at least an equal position. O is certainly tempting the fates by accepting the double: First he must survive the attack and the possibility of being gammoned, and then he must try to win a game in which he will never be a clear-cut favorite in the foreseeable future.

Let's return again to X's play 6/4*/1*. X would have preferred to point on O's blot on the four point; however, since he is unable to do so, he hits two men. As a rule, hitting two opposing men is a strong play even when it requires leaving a blot in your inner board. Such a play always keeps your opponent off balance since his entire roll is then required to re-enter (unless he rolls doubles). Furthermore, O is not a favorite to re-enter with *both* men even though there are only two points closed in X's inner board. X hits two men to capitalize on the early positional advantage he has gained. By keeping the momentum of the attack going, he hopes that O will never have a chance to consolidate his own position.

There are several conditions which indicate the advisability of making an aggressive play:

1. You hold an advanced anchor in your opponent's inner board. Here X holds O's five point. We cannot stress the importance of this point too highly.

2. You have closed more points in your inner board than your opponent. Here X holds two inner-board points, O one. Whenever embarking on a variation where an exchange of hits is possible or likely, the relative number of inner-board points is an important consideration. The player with more points closed will always be at an advantage since his opponent will be more likely to have difficulty re-entering. Even staying out once may be fatal, especially without the protection of an advanced anchor.

3. Blots in your opponent's inner board tend to make attacking more desirable because of the possibility of return shots. Here O has a blot on the twenty-one point. Since O has two men on the bar, there is no possible roll (except doubles) on which O can both re-enter and simultaneously cover his blot. Therefore, even if O re-enters on the one point hitting X, X will have a direct return shot at O's twenty-one-point blot.

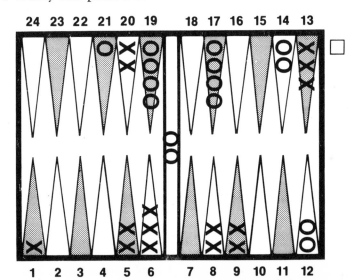

Roll 4 for O
O to Play 6–3
(X 3–2 6/4*/1*)

O moves bar/3, ø.

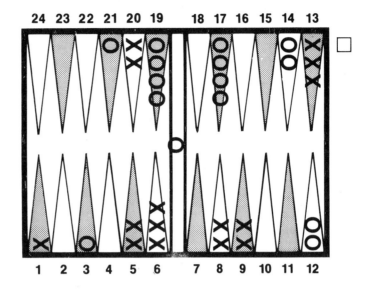

Roll 5 for X
X to Play 6–5
(O 6–3 bar/3, Ø)

X moves 9/3*, 8/3, pointing on O's head and continuing the attack. By making your points in order (beginning with the points furthest from home), you assure yourself of a superior position even if your opponent survives the attack and makes an anchor. Should O manage to make the one point in this position, he will still have great difficulty getting past X's blockade.

Let's consider what might happen if X foolishly decides to cover the one point and hit the blot 9/3*, 6/1. Now O is forced to re-enter on the two, three, or four point. If he succeeds in making one of these points — particularly the three or four point — X will be in a weaker position. The men on the one point are out of play.

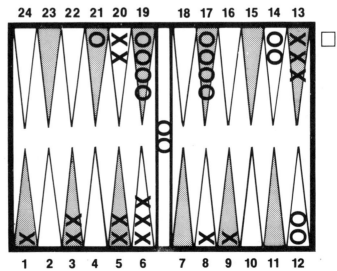

Roll 5 for O
O to Play 4–3
(X 6–5 4/3*, 8/3)

O moves bar/4, ø. This move is forced. O is faced with a grim struggle for survival and hopes to establish a foothold somewhere in X's board to avoid being closed out completely. Every additional point that X closes makes O more desperate. The outcome of the game will depend on the next few critical rolls.

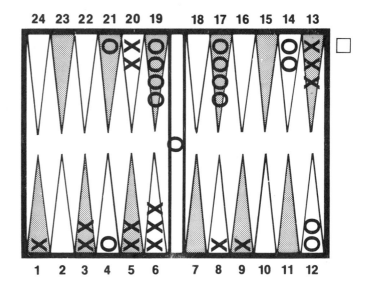

Roll 6 for X
X to Play 5–4
(O 4–3 bar/4, Ø)

X moves 9/4*, 8/4, pointing on O again and putting a second man on the bar. X closes the four point rather than the one point in order to make his points in order. Owning the three, four, five, and six points will make X a favorite in the game even if O manages to survive the blitz.

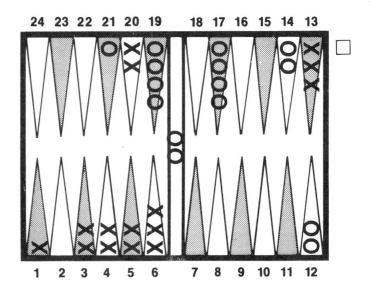

Roll 6 for O
O to Play 4–1
(X 5–4 9/4*, 8/4)

O moves bar/1*, ø, finally hitting the blot on the one point. Notice, however, that since X doubled he has kept pounding O constantly and left him no opportunity to move any men other than his back runners: O's other checkers haven't moved since the third roll of the game! Since O has been too busy to cover the blot on the twenty-one point, X now has a direct 4-shot at it.

Roll 7 for X
X to Play 6–1
(O 4–1 bar/1*, Ø)

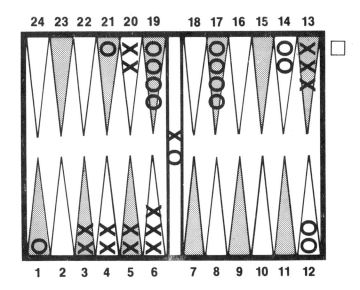

X moves bar/24, 13/7. X brings more ammunition into the battle by moving a new builder to his bar point. X's primary strategy is to continue his attack — he can afford to wait until later to bring his back men out. By playing to the bar point 13/7, X threatens to establish a powerful 5-point prime from the three point to the seven point. Even if O rolls a 1 and establishes an anchor on the one point, he will still be hopelessly trapped. In any case, X should win the game easily.

Roll 7 for O
O to Play 3–3
(X 6–1 bar/24, 13/7)

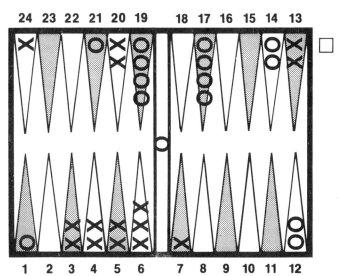

O ø.

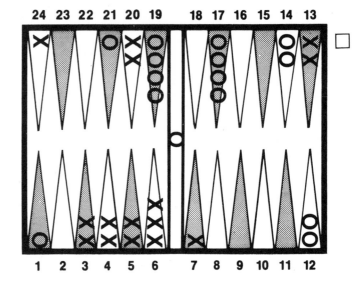

Roll 8 for X
X to Play 4–4
(O 3–3 Ø)

X moves 13/1*, 13/9. Once again X presses his attack. X could have hit O's second man without leaving a blot by **switching points,** that is, by moving both men off the five point and making the one point 5/1(2). Switching points can be an effective strategy in some cases, especially when rolling small doubles.

Here, however, it would be extremely unwise to play 5/1(2). We have seen that even if O is fortunate enough to survive the attack, X's 4- or 5-point prime will still assure X of an almost certain win. Should X make the structurally unsound play of breaking his prime by relinquishing the five point for the one point, then O might win if he survives the blitz. There is no reason not to play soundly in case O, for example, should come in with a double. X need not worry about being hit on the one point; O has only a 1-point board with a blot and X still maintains his advanced anchor.

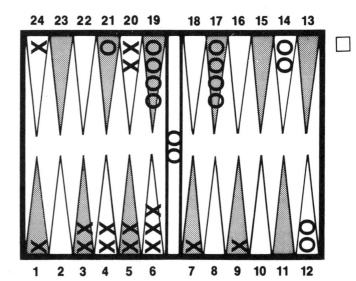

Roll 8 for O
O to Play 3–2
(X 4–4 13/1*, 13/9)

O moves bar/2, ø.

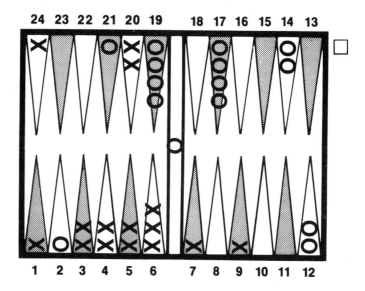

Roll 9 for X
X to Play 4–1
(O 3–2 bar/2, Ø)

X moves 6/2*/1. With one checker X simultaneously hits another man and covers his own blot, creating a 5-point board. O is now in his death throes — he is no longer favored to come in with even one man, much less two. Only a miraculous roll 2–2 will enable him to survive.

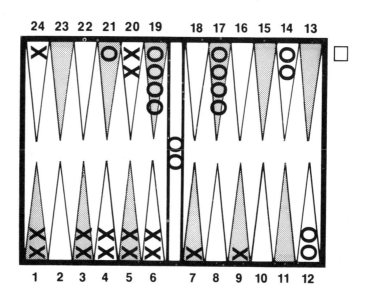

Roll 9 for O
O to Play 6–5
(X 4–1 6/2*/1)

O ø.

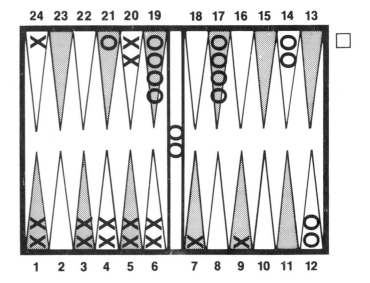

Roll 10 for X
X to Play 3–2
(O 6–5 Ø)

X moves 9/6, 20/18. X has passed up the opportunity to hit O again and to cover his bar point, 24/21*, 9/7, which would make a 5-point prime. He has also given up the twenty point. Has X gone mad??

No. X is no longer interested in a 5-point prime; his main concern is to complete the close-out. X wants to be able to hit O on the two point should he re-enter. By using the 3 to bring a man into the six point 9/6, X creates a second builder bearing directly on the two point. The idea here is to either make the two point directly on one roll, or to hit O on the two point if he re-enters and then cover the point if he fails to come in.

What about 24/21*? It is not really necessary for X to hit the blot on the twenty-one point; if X completes the close-out, he will easily be in a position to gammon O since O has not advanced far from the starting position with most of his men. If X wishes, he can probably hit this blot later at his leisure.

However, for technical reasons to be discussed later, if X closes O out and begins to bear off, it is probably safer for him with only two men on the bar rather than three. Hitting the third man may actually be a liability.

X can now afford to give up the twenty point because he is not in immediate danger. With two men on the bar against a 5-point board, O no longer presents a threat.

As a general rule, whenever your opponent has two or more men on the bar (whether you have a 5-point board or not), you should not be concerned about blots outside your inner board. Remember that even if your opponent rolls a good number, he must use the full roll to bring both his men in (with the exception of doubles, which would enable him to move elsewhere as well). He therefore has no numbers left to hit you with. When your opponent has two men on the bar, then, take advantage of this opportunity to deploy your men well and diversify your builders.

The indicated play 9/6, 20/18 is also superior to an alternate play 9/6, 24/22 for a technical reason. Let's compare the positions which result from both plays.

Correct Play: Roll 10 for X
(X 3–2 9/6, 20/18)

Alternate Move: Roll 10 for X
(X 3–2 9/6, 24/22)

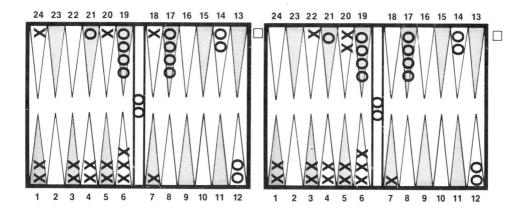

What would happen if your next roll was 3–3?

If you had played 9/6, 24/22, your three back men would be unable to move. You would be forced to take the entire roll with your remaining men. In order to maintain a 5-point board, you would have to switch points 5/2(2) and play 7/1, **killing a checker** (that is, taking it permanently out of play).

By correctly moving 9/6, 20/18, you can see that 3–3 subsequently plays without having to give up the five point or kill a man.

It is important to be aware of freak rolls which could destroy your position on the next move.

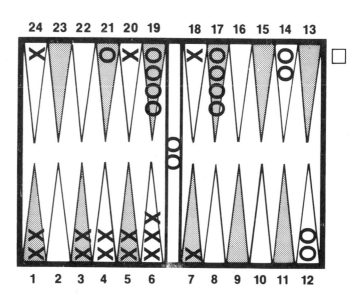

Roll 10 for O
O to Play 6–5
(X 3–2 9/6, 20/18)

O ∅.

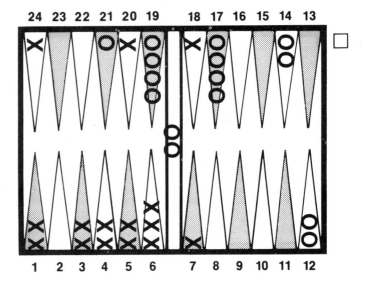

Roll 11 for X
X to Play 5–5
(O 6–5 Ø)

X moves 18/8, 20/10, bearing on the two point with a third builder. A player impatient for the close-out might slot a man 7/2 hoping to cover on the next roll if O stays out. It is seldom correct to slot with two men on the bar. The proper procedure is to wait until your opponent comes in and *then* hit him with a blot if necessary.

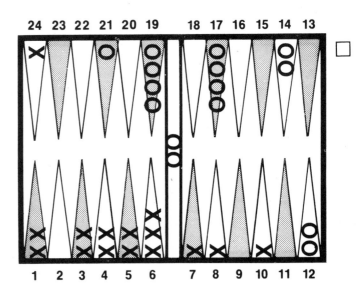

Roll 11 for O
O to Play 5–2
(X 5–5 18/8, 20/10)

O moves bar/2, ø.

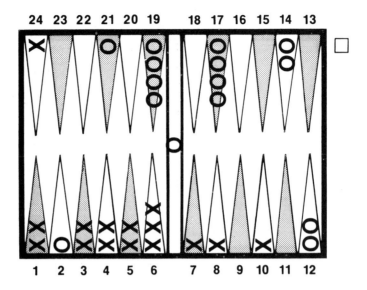

Roll 12 for X
X to Play 3–1
(O 5–2 bar/2, Ø)

X moves 6/2*. X hits the blot, trying to close O out. This is more important than hitting the blot on the twenty-one point (see discussion after Roll 10). The best — and in the long run safest — strategy is to complete the close-out and deny O an anchor to fight from.

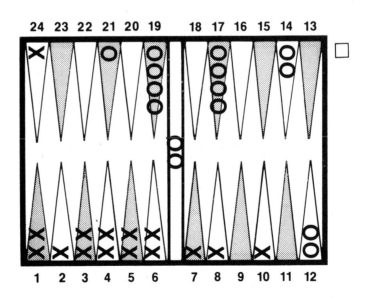

Roll 12 for O
O to Play 5–1
(X 3–1 6/2*)

O ø.

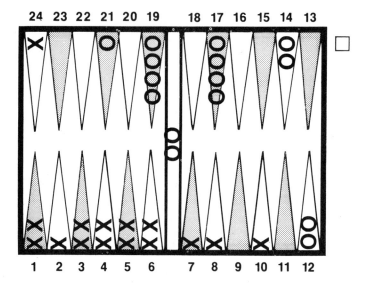

Roll 13 for X
X to Play 6–4
(O 5–1 Ø)

X moves 8/2, 24/20. X completes the close-out and now starts to extricate his back man. X is not interested in waiting to pick up O's blot. By bringing his last man home and bearing off carefully, X should easily win a gammon.

You should review the rules for a successful bear-off against opposition given after Game II and then roll the rest of the game out yourself to practice the bear-off technique. Barring an unlikely accident, O should be gammoned. He will lose four points instead of the one point he would have lost had he passed the double.

Game IV Summary

1. The single most important point to control in the middle game is the opponent's five point (called the **golden point**). This advanced anchor usually gives a strong measure of security throughout the game. With this security, you may be able to make plays that are otherwise too dangerous. A common error of the average player is to fail to make this point, or to relinquish it prematurely.

2. The following are some important factors which motivate aggressive plays:

    A. You hold an advanced anchor.

    B. You have more points closed in your inner board than your opponent.

    C. There are enemy blots lying around the board which may be hit before your opponent recovers from your attack and can safety them. Opposing blots in your opponent's home board offer prospects for return shots if you are hit.

3. If there is a chance of being gammoned, be especially cautious about accepting doubles.

4. It is risky to move up in your opponent's inner board when he has extra builders in his outer and/or inner boards.

5. Hitting two men in your inner board is a strong play even when you must leave a blot to do so. It keeps your opponent off balance and allows you to move freely elsewhere.

6. When launching an all-out attack, it is sometimes correct to make deep points — especially if this leaves your opponent on the bar against a strong inner board. However, if you have a choice, making the higher point in your inner board is preferable. Making points in the proper order may guarantee a strong game should your attack fail.

7. When your opponent has two or more men on the bar, concentrate primarily on bringing builders to bear on your inner board — not on safety-ing blots outside your inner board.

8. Technical close-out procedures:

A. The best technical procedure for closing out an opponent is usu-ally *not* to slot if he has two or more men on the bar.

B. Move carefully when your opponent is closed out and you wish to bring your remaining men into your inner board. Try not to expose yourself to those doubles that will leave your outside men blocked, thus forcing you to break your inner board prematurely.

C. When your opponent is closed out and the gammon seems a certainty, avoid hitting extra men since this will increase the possibility of trouble in the bear-off.

CHAPTER 10.
THE BACKGAME

The backgame is perhaps the most fascinating area of backgammon. It is certainly one of the most difficult. If played properly, it may enable you to become a strong favorite in what otherwise would be a hopelessly lost position. Let's look at the overall strategy of the backgame first.

The fundamental prerequisite for a backgame is to establish at least two points in your opponent's inner board. (In rare and usually favorable cases, you may be able to establish more than two points.) It is usually necessary to hold two points which are close together and deep in your opponent's inner board. We shall see which points are the best to maintain.

The second part of the basic game plan is to allow O to bring his men around the board and to begin the bear-in process. As he bears in, he will, necessarily, have to abandon whatever prime he may have. He may have to give up key points in his inner board and pile up his remaining men awkwardly on his remaining points. After he weakens his position in this way, you hope to reach the third stage.

In the third stage, you expect your opponent to be forced to repeatedly leave shots until you hit him. We have already noted that it is hard to bear off safely even against a 1-point game; bearing off safely without ever having to leave a shot against two deep inner board points is almost impossible. Since each shot that is left will probably be a double shot, you can reasonably expect to carry out stage three successfully.

The fourth stage is to win the game by containing the man you have hit (and possibly hitting another man). Because your opponent in the second stage presumably has already broken his prime, taken men out of play, and sometimes even broken points in his inner board, he will be unable to fight back successfully.

It is critical not to take any men out of play while waiting for the opportunity to hit. In particular you must avoid piling them on the one and two points at all costs, since all your men are needed to win the game after hitting. Remember, the key to a successful backgame is to give yourself enough time to play your remaining men (without killing any) while waiting for shots. It is around this issue — timing — that all the vital maneuvering and strategy takes place. The issue of timing can be extraordinarily complicated. Let's look at the stages through which a typical backgame goes.

Illustrative Game

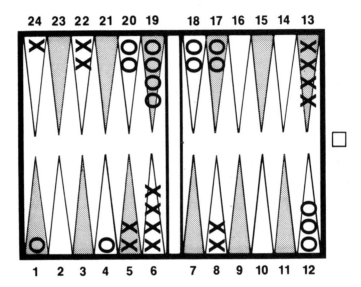

Position 1
X to Play 6–2

In Position 1, X has fallen behind and begins to consider the possibility of playing a backgame. He has not committed himself to a backgame yet; he lacks a second point in O's inner board, without which a backgame is impossible. The correct play is 13/7, 6/4*, attacking and making one last attempt to win the game by going forward.

24 23 22 21 20 19   18 17 16 15 14 13

Position 2
X to Play 5–2

1   2   3   4   5   6   7   8   9 10 11 12

A few moves later, we see that the attack has failed: O has hit X and escaped one of his back runners. X has established a second point and is ready to go into a full backgame. Indeed, in this position, it would be a mistake to try to win the game otherwise.

In Position 2, the correct play is 8/3*, 6/4. X no longer hopes to successfully attack or contain O — in fact, he hopes to be hit. By being hit, he may be able to bring a man back into O's inner board and then around the entire circuit. In this way, X will give himself more *time*. By continually recirculating his men in this manner, X avoids running out of time and having either to relinquish one of the two key points or kill men. Because X wishes to be hit and sent back, the overall strategic plan has been called "retreat to victory."

At this point, O unwisely doubles, and X accepts. O is forced to hit X twice before getting out of X's inner board. A few moves later, Position 3 is reached.

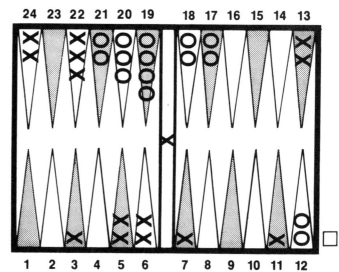

24 23 22 21 20 19   18 17 16 15 14 13

Position 3
X to Play 5–1

1   2   3   4   5   6   7   8   9 10 11 12

X stayed out on the previous roll. Ordinarily, this is bad, but when playing a backgame, it is favorable since you gain time by not moving. The correct move in Position 12 is bar/24, 13/8. You purposely leave an additional blot as bait for O. O should avoid hitting you if possible. He hopes to roll small numbers and come home slowly. *The key to defeating a backgame is to spoil your opponent's timing.*

A few rolls later, Position 4 is reached:

**Position 4
X to Play 5–2**

O is closer to home and appears to have X hopelessly trapped. X, however, is actually a favorite in this position; he plays 24/22, 13/8. It is crucial that X not hit O now. Remember, the object at this time is *not* to prevent O from getting home safely. In fact, X wants O to come home quickly and break up his prime. Only after O breaks his prime can X consider trying to win the game while going forward. To hit and try to contain the hit man, *and* also escape all five of his back men from behind a 5-point prime, is a near-impossibility.

Position 5
O to Play 5–4, then
X to Play 4–3

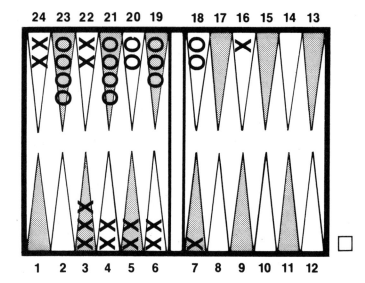

In Position 4, it is important that X play his 2 up to the twenty-two point. The object of having extra men sent back is to enable him to gain time by bringing them around the board. In order to ensure being able to escape and bring them back around, it is mandatory for X to bring the spare men up to his most advanced point in O's inner board.

Soon Position 5 is reached: O has awkwardly stacked men on his two and four points, while X has begun building a strong position on his side of the board. In order to win, X must not only make a strong position, but, more importantly, he must also be able to hold it. The vital time gained by having two extra men hit enabled X to reach the present position now instead of many rolls earlier. The spare man on the sixteen point is crucial since X may still have to wait a few more rolls until O gives him a shot.

We now assume O rolls 5–4. He is forced to play 18/23, 19/23, leaving a man on his bar point exposed to a double shot. Since O's prime is gone, X is prepared to hit. Even if X misses the double shot, he will almost certainly get more shots later. Fortunately, he rolls 4–3 and plays 22/18*, 16/13, preparing to make his bar point. O stays out. X doubles, and O must pass.

CHAPTER 11.
PIP COUNT

SINCE BACKGAMMON IS essentially a race to move all your men around and off the board before your opponent, being able to determine your relative position in this race is often essential. Although you can make an approximate determination by eye, sometimes this is not accurate enough.

A more precise method is to count pips. This counting, though annoying and tedious at times, is essential to determine your standing in the race — especially where the position is at all complicated.

Three methods for making the count follow.

Pip Count Methods

Direct Method

A player bringing his checkers home in a race wants to do so in the most economical way. The **pip count** represents the difference between the total number of points each player must roll in order to take all his checkers off the board, assuming that no pips are wasted. By *wasted*, we mean that no number higher than necessary is used to bear a man off.

The number of pips represented by *each checker* is simply the number point the checker is on, *counting 1 as the first point in each player's home board.* For X, a checker on the five point is 5 pips, two on the ten point are 20 pips, one on the sixteen point is 16 pips, and so on. (Since the twenty-four point counts as 1 for O, an O checker on the twenty point is 5 pips, two on the fifteen point are 20 pips, one on the nine point is 16 pips.)

To compute your total number of pips (*not* the same as the pip count), you add up the pips of all your checkers. Then you add up the pips of your opponent's checkers. The difference between these two sums indicates whether you are *ahead* or *behind* in pips, and by how much. This is called the **pip count**. By *ahead*, we mean the player who has the *lower* number of pips, and thus is closer to home; by *behind*, we mean the player who has the *higher* number of pips, and thus is further from home.

A full example of the direct method of pip counting is given below:

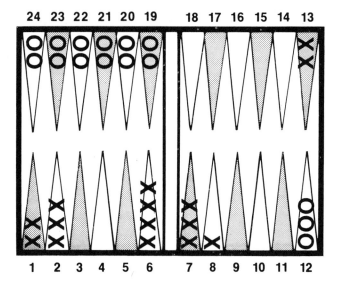

Position 1

X's Count
Two men on the one point = 2 × 1 = 2
Three men on the two point = 3 × 2 = 6
Four men on the six point = 4 × 6 = 24
Three men on the seven point = 3 × 7 = 21
One man on the eight point = 1 × 8 = 8
Two men on the thirteen point = 2 × 13 = 26

X's total is 87 pips. X needs 87 points rolled on the dice to bear his men off, assuming that no numbers are wasted.

O's Count
Remember that for O we count the twenty-four point as 1, twenty-three as 2, etc.
Two men on O's one point = 2 × 1 = 2
Two men on O's two point = 2 × 2 = 4
Two men on O's three point = 2 × 3 = 6
Two men on O's four point = 2 × 4 = 8
Two men on O's five point = 2 × 5 = 10
Two men on O's six point = 2 × 6 = 12
Three men on O's thirteen point = 3 × 13 = 39

O's total is 81 pips. X's total is 87 pips. X is 6 pips further from bringing his men off the board than O. X is 6 pips *behind* O.

Saving Time
To count quickly, it is useful to memorize the positions of the points which represent 10, 13, and 20 pips for each player. Also, keep in mind that a closed board with two men on each inner board point equals 42 pips.

Various mental exercises also make the calculations go faster. Here is a symmetry trick: If point A and point B have the same number of men *and* are separated by an odd number of points, the total number of pips on A + B would equal the total number of pips on the central point, C, if all the men were there. For example, if you have three men on the nine point and three men on the eleven point, you have a total of $(3 \times 9) + (3 \times 11) = 60$ pips. This is equal to six men on the ten point $(6 \times 10) = 60$ pips.

Another trick is to omit counting the number of men on a point if your opponent has the same number of men on the corresponding point. In Position 1, both X and O have two men on their respective one points. If we omit counting either point, the 2 pips lost by each player will cancel out and the final pip count will be the same.

Comparison Method

This method of finding the pip count gives us the same result as the direct method. It provides a running total of the pip count. The comparison method is preferable to the direct method because it eliminates the need to figure out and then compare two separately totaled sums.

Using the comparison method, you compare the number of checkers that you and your opponent have on corresponding points. You subtract the number of men your opponent has from the number of men you have. Then you multiply this difference by the number of the point you are comparing. You now have a pip count for a particular point. If you have more checkers on the point than your opponent, you will end up with a plus pip count; if you have less, you will end up with a minus pip count for that particular point.

As you compare each pair of points in turn, you keep a running total of the pip counts for each point, subtracting a pip count when you have less pips than your opponent, and adding when you have more. When you have finished comparing the sets of points, the final running total will indicate the complete pip count for the entire position. If it is plus, you are behind; if it is minus, you are ahead.

Let's use the comparison method to determine the pip count in Position 1.

Point #	# of X men on point	# of O men on point	#X men minus #O men	col. 4 x col. 1	X's running total of pip count
one	2	2	$2 - 2 = 0$	$0 \times 1 = 0$	0 (even)
two	3	2	$3 - 2 = +1$	$1 \times 2 = +2$	+2
three	0	2	$0 - 2 = -2$	$-2 \times 3 = -6$	$+2 - 6 = -4$
four	0	2	$0 - 2 = -2$	$-2 \times 4 = -8$	$-4 - 8 = -12$
five	0	2	$0 - 2 = -2$	$-2 \times 5 = -10$	$-12 - 10 = -22$
six	4	2	$4 - 2 = +2$	$2 \times 6 = +12$	$-22 + 12 = -10$
seven	3	0	$3 - 0 = +3$	$3 \times 7 = +21$	$-10 + 21 = +11$
eight	1	0	$1 - 0 = +1$	$1 \times 8 = +8$	$+11 + 8 = +19$
thirteen	2	3	$2 - 3 = -1$	$-1 \times 13 = -13$	$+19 - 13 = +6$

The final total indicates that X is +6, or 6 pips *behind* in the race against O.

Experience has shown that the comparison method is usually quicker and more reliable than the direct method — especially when the positions of the two players are similar.

Mental Shift Method

This method is a modification of the comparison method. In this case you mentally move men of one player to make a position identical with the other player. Then you count the number of pips you had to move each checker to make the positions identical. If you have to move your men toward your home board, you add the number of pips; if you have to move your men away from your home board, you subtract the number of pips moved.

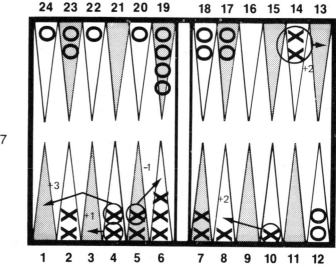

Position 2
2 +2 − 1 + 3 + 1 = 7

In Position 2, we have indicated how a few of X's men may be rearranged to yield identical positions with O. In order to make the positions identical, we must move X's men a net total of 7 pips forward, so therefore X is 7 pips *behind* in the race.

The advantage of this method is obvious — with practically no work or calculation, you get the total pip count in a matter of seconds. For those who hate having to remember and total long strings of numbers, as the author does, this is a real blessing.

The disadvantage is that there is no set way of determining which checkers to move to make the positions identical. Furthermore, there may be many different ways to shift the men to arrive at identical positions.

To determine when to use this method, study various positions and find the one where the fewest checkers need be moved to make X's and O's positions identical. When the two positions are entirely dissimilar, the number of men to be shifted may well make this method more trouble than it is worth. With practice, however, it is often surprising how few checkers have to be moved to equate the positions.

(Note: It is permissible to mentally rearrange your opponent's checkers. If you move his forward, you subtract the number of pips; if you move them backward, away from his home board, you add the number of pips.)

You can facilitate counting even in very dissimilar positions by mentally moving a few men so that opposing men will cancel out, and, keeping track of the pips you moved, do the rest of the counting by one of the other methods.

The next four positions can be used to practice the mental shift method.

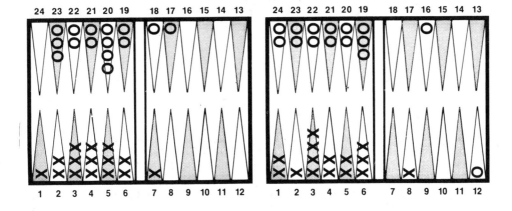

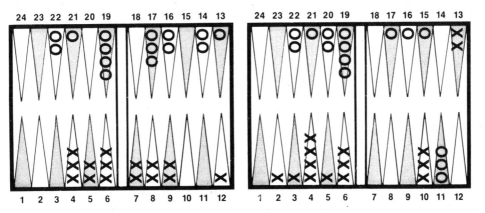

Positions 3A, 4A, 5A, and 6A each illustrate one possible rearrangement to quickly find the total pip count.

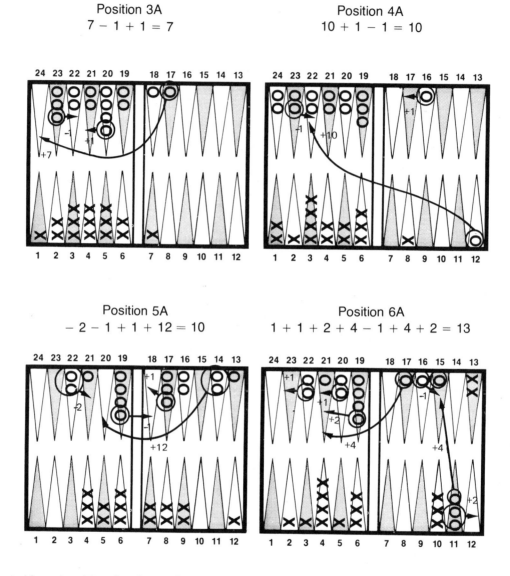

Position 3A
$$7 - 1 + 1 = 7$$

Position 4A
$$10 + 1 - 1 = 10$$

Position 5A
$$- 2 - 1 + 1 + 12 = 10$$

Position 6A
$$1 + 1 + 2 + 4 - 1 + 4 + 2 = 13$$

Keeping Track of the Count

Once you enter into a race, there may be several occasions when it is necessary to know what the exact pip count is. Rather than recalculating it every time, it is usually easier to keep a running total. After the pip count has been made, you may readjust it after each roll by the number of pips actually rolled on the dice.

Begin with the pip count figure. Remember that if it is minus you are ahead, and if plus, behind. If you are 8 pips ahead and you roll 3–2 (or 5 pips), you are now 13 pips ahead. Your opponent then rolls 5–4 (9 pips), so you are now 13 minus 9 = 4 pips ahead. You roll 2–2 (8 pips) and are now 12 pips ahead. He rolls 4–4 (16 pips), so now you are 4 pips behind, etc.

Evaluating the Race

In backgammon, the average number of pips thrown on a roll of the dice is $8^1/_6$; it isn't 7, as one might expect, because of the special rule for playing doubles. If you wish to see how many *rolls* ahead or behind you are, simply take the total pip count and divide by 8 (dividing by 8 is not only easier than $8^1/_6$, but actually gives you a better indication). If, for example, you are 20 pips ahead in the race, $^{20}/_8 = 2^1/_2$ tells you that you are $2^1/_2$ rolls ahead in the race.

If you are on roll, what pip count would constitute an even race?

If the pip count were exactly even, the player on roll would have the advantage.

It is sometimes wrongly maintained that being on roll compensates for being 8 pips behind. Assume, however, that you get an average roll. The pip count will now be even. Now your opponent has the advantage because he is on roll with an even count.

The correct answer is that if you are 4 pips behind *and* on roll the position is even. If you then roll an average 8 pips, your opponent comes on roll, like you, 4 pips behind.

Offering and Accepting Doubles

How many pips ahead should you be to double? And how many behind to accept?

Many authorities disagree on the exact number of pips needed. Rather than give an exact mathematical formula (which most players would probably never bother to use), we offer a simple rule of thumb, along with a discussion of its limitations and exceptions.

Number of pips you have	Minimum pips ahead to double	Maximum allowable pips behind to accept
Medium-length race (about 60)	7	10
Long race (about 100)	10	13

In most races you will never have exactly 60 or 100 pips, so modifications must be made. The longer the race, the more pips needed to double and the more pips behind you can be to take. In a 90-pip race, for example, slightly less than 10 pips ahead are needed to double, and slightly less than 13 behind allow you to take. Some races are even longer than 100 pips, in which case higher numbers would be used.

Although this rule may seem imprecise, it is the one actually used by the author and several other knowledgeable players. The exact number of pips remaining in the game is not emphasized because it is often easier to find the total pip count using the comparison or shift method. Unlike the direct method, however, the other methods do not give the actual number of pips remaining on both sides — only the difference in the two pip totals. When using the comparison method, then, a rough evaluation of the race will usually suffice. Misevaluating the *length* of the race even by as much as 10 or 15 pips is unlikely to change your doubling decision significantly. Since the doubling rules given are approximations anyway, the actual equity lost in the game will be negligible.

In contrast, miscounting the total pip count by even a small amount may contribute to a significant misassessment. In a long race, for example, a mistake of 5 pips in the pip count could drastically alter your decision to double: If you thought you were ahead only 9 pips, you would not double, whereas if you were ahead 14 pips, you would not only double, but your opponent might pass!

The doubling criteria were given in terms of a "medium-length race" and a "long race," by which we meant races with about 60 and 100 pips remaining. The exact length of the race is not important, so we shall give some rough criteria which will enable you to look at a position to approximately determine its length.

A medium-length race may be thought of as one in which almost all the men are relatively smoothly distributed in the inner board and the bear-off is about to begin. Since there are fifteen men, the "average" checker will be on the four point in a medium-length race.

A long race may be thought of as one in which there are usually three or four rolls left until the bear-off can begin. Or a long race would be one in which the men are evenly distributed about the bar, that is, there are about the same number of pips needed to reach the bar from the men in the outer boards as there would be from the men in the inner boards.

To give you an idea of what medium- and long-length races look like, look back at Positions 3, 4, 5, and 6. In Positions 3 and 4, X has exactly 60 pips, and in Positions 5 and 6, X has 100 pips.

In order to apply the rules for accepting and refusing doubles, you must know the exact pip count. You may wish to practice the pip count in these four positions to determine what the correct doubling strategy is. Any method for counting may be used; the mental shift method is the one illustrated in Positions 3A, 4A, 5A, and 6A.

In Position 3, X is 7 pips ahead. He should double and O should accept. This constitutes the minimum lead with which X should double here.

In Position 4, X is 10 pips ahead. X should double and O should still take. However, this is a borderline take for O; if he were any further behind, he would refuse.

In Position 5, X is 10 pips ahead and should double; O takes. If X had any smaller lead, he should probably wait to double.

In Position 6, X is 13 pips ahead and doubles; O has a borderline take.

In races such as those in Positions 3, 4, 5, and 6, the pip count is a highly reliable indicator of the standing in the race. There are positions, however, where the pip count alone may be somewhat misleading and appropriate modifications must be made. Consider the following situations:

1. In applying our doubling rule based on the pip count, a distinction must be made between a first double and a re-double. You should be slightly freer about doubling when the cube is in the middle, and slightly more conservative if you own the cube.

Owning the cube and being, therefore, the only person able to double, gives you an increased equity in the game. By re-doubling you give up this equity, whereas if the cube is in the middle you have less to lose since you are not the sole owner.

2. The way your men are distributed has a bearing on the race. When there are gaps in your inner board, you are more likely to miss taking men off (thus wasting pips). You should especially avoid leaving gaps on your four or five point. If you are unable to avoid bearing in with a stripped four or five point, your position will probably be somewhat worse than the pip count indicates.

3. Your bear-off will also be adversely affected if you have too many men piled on points deep in your inner board. If (taking an extreme case) you had four men on your one point while your opponent had only one man on his six point, obviously your 2-pip lead in the race would mean nothing. What matters is the *number of rolls left to complete the bear-off*.

Whenever a bear-off has begun in a short race, and each side has several men off, it is easiest to evaluate the position by estimating the probable number of *rolls* each side has left.

Position 7

In a medium-length or long race, having men piled on your one and two points will also adversely affect your chances. The reason for this is that eventually large numbers will probably be used to remove men from the one and two points and pips will be wasted. The pip count will be misleading when many pips are wasted, or when there are gaps in the inner board.

In Position 7, the pip count is exactly even, but O's men are better distributed. O has a gap on the five point which could potentially cause trouble, but fortunately he has a few rolls to rectify this before the bear-off begins. O should therefore make every attempt to bear into the five point and not to the six point to avoid leaving this gap.

X, on the other hand, already has men piled on his one point, and there is nothing he can do about this. Inevitably this will cause pips to be wasted in the bear-off. If you wish numerically to compensate for this in terms of the pip count, imagine that three of the surplus men on the one point are on the three point instead. This gives a more realistic count of 83 for X.

Pip Count Applications

Holding Positions

The pip count is primarily applied in racing positions where no further contact is possible. There is, therefore, little point in keeping track of the pip count in typical middle-game positions where there is little chance of the game's evolving directly into a pure race. Occasionally, however, a holding position may arise in which there is a significant chance of the game's being completed with no further contact. In such positions, the prospects for winning the race may determine the correct play.

In this position, the only possible remaining contact involves the men on the ten and fifteen points.

Problem A: O rolls 2–2. How would you play this number?

Position 8
(A) O to Play 2–2
(B) X to Play 2–2

Without bothering with an exact pip count, O realizes he is far ahead. Therefore, the correct play is 10/14(2) effectively eliminating further contact and leaving O a clear winner.

Problem B: X rolls 2–2. How would you play this number?

X has almost no chance in a straight race and his only hope is that O will have trouble clearing the ten point. Therefore, X plays 7/3, 8/4 and keeps his two men back on the fifteen point. These two men serve to *hold* O's men on the ten point. Eventually O must move these men. If O does not roll a double which would enable him to move them together, he will eventually have to move one of them, leaving X a direct shot.

Since X is behind in the race, he tries to hold O. Since O is ahead, however, he has no desire to hold X but merely wants to come home safely. In order to know who's holding whom, you must know the leader in the race. In Position 8, a simple inspection can determine who is ahead.

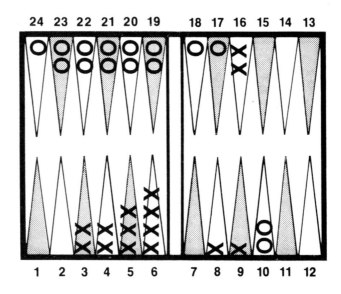

Position 9
X to Play 3–3

In Position 9, the relative standing in the race after X takes the 3–3 is sufficiently close to warrant a pip count. Fortunately, X's and O's positions may easily be compared by mentally rearranging the men as shown in Position 9A to show that X is 16 pips behind as the position stands *before* the roll.

Therefore, *after* X's move, O will be 16 minus 12 = 4 pips ahead and on roll — a clear-cut favorite in the race.

Since X is behind, he wishes to hold O as effectively as possible and so chooses to stay on the sixteen point, 6 pips in front of O's two men on the ten point. Since O is ahead, he does not want to hold X — he just wants to get home safely and will run at the first opportunity with a double (except 6–6).

What will happen if O remains ahead in the race and neither player rolls a double? Eventually, one of the players (probably O since he is ahead) will be forced to break the point in the outfield, leaving a man exposed. This will happen when a player is unable to legally play his move in his inner board, in

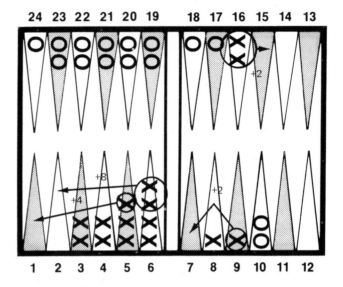

Position 9A
2 + 2 + 8 + 4 = 16

particular when he has no other 6's to play except with his outside point. For this reason, both players must attempt to conserve as many 6's as possible. Each player here has two spare 6's; the third 6 rolled by either side will force a shot.

Returning to Position 9, we see that X should not move forward off the sixteen point and should not bring the men on the eight and nine points into the inner board. The exact play with the remaining men is not critically important, but the best play is probably 4/1(2), 6/3, 5/2.

A subtler version of the same ideas (who's holding whom) is shown in Position 10.

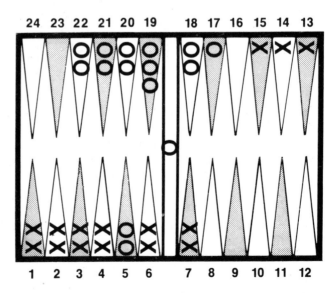

Position 10
X to Play 3–2

Even many experienced players make their eleven point, 14/11, 13/11. This is a serious mistake; the correct play is 15/12, 14/12.

In this position, X is clearly far ahead in the race so he wants to get home safely and doesn't want to hold O back. In Game IV we emphasized that the best single point to hold when you want to block your opponent is the point 6 pips in front of him. However, X has no desire to restrain O's men on the five point and, therefore, no reason to make his eleven point. In fact, if X makes the eleven point and O re-enters, O will be holding X because the eleven point is difficult to clear without leaving a direct shot. Rather than being an asset for X, the eleven point will be an enormous liability.

The correct play, 15/12, 14/12, presents no such problems. Even when O re-enters, clearing the twelve point will at worst involve only leaving an indirect 7-shot.

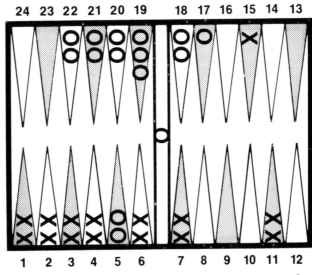

Position 11
X to Play 3–2

In Position 11, X has a 3–2 to play. Moving 15/10 so you are only exposed to 5–5 is a common error. While this is the safest immediate play, the real problem in this position is to clear the eleven point safely. Maintaining the eleven point can be fatal on the next roll if O re-enters. It will then be hard to clear without leaving a direct shot.

The correct play is 11/6. Since O is on the bar, X seizes this opportunity to clear the eleven point immediately. The risk of being hit with a 6–5 is more than compensated by the fact that you are clearing a potentially dangerous point.

Another common variant of the same theme is illustrated in Position 12.

The pip count reveals that after X plays 2–1 he will still be 4 pips behind despite the fact that O still has two men back. Because X is behind in the race, he wishes to make it as difficult as possible for O to escape and plays 6/3, maintaining 4 points in front of O.

Let's look at a different problem using the same position. How would O play 2–1?

Playing 18/20, 19/20, making the twenty point would be a dangerous mistake. O wants to leave X's five point with *both* men to maintain his lead in the race — leaving with a single man would be very dangerous. If he plays 18/20, he will be forced to run with one man if he rolls a 6 (except 6–6, 6–5), leaving

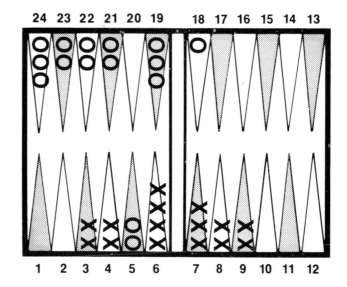

Position 12
(A) X to Play 2–1
(B) O to Play 2–1

the remaining man to X's tender mercies. If, on the other hand, O correctly takes his whole roll within his inner board 19/22, he will be able to move the man on the eighteen point if he rolls a bad 6 and will not be forced to run from the five point prematurely.

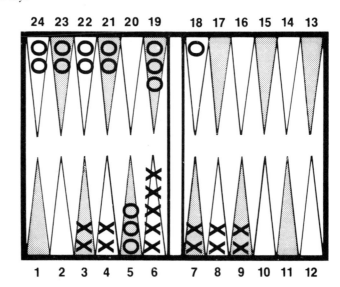

Position 13
(A) X to Play 2–1
(B) O to Play 2–1

In contrast, X will have a 16-pip lead after his roll in Position 13. With a clearly favorable race, X need not worry about containing O — his chief concern is bearing his men in as safely as possible. Towards this end, X plays 9/8, 9/7, following the principles outlined in Game II for safe bear-in: Clear the points furthest from home and avoid leaving gaps. In Position 13, if O rolled 2–1 the correct play would be 19/20, 18/20, giving O a closed board. O has no reason to save 6's because he has a third man on the five point to run with a 6.

CHAPTER 12.
BASIC ODDS

LET US EXAMINE the structure of a single roll of two dice. There are 36 possible combinations of the dice, as listed in Table 1.

Table 1. Combinations of the Dice

Dice Roll	Number of Combinations	Dice Roll	Number of Combinations
1–1	1	2–3, or 3–2	2
2–2	1	2–4, or 4–2	2
3–3	1	2–5, or 5–2	2
4–4	1	2–6, or 6–2	2
5–5	1	3–4, or 4–3	2
6–6	1	3–5, or 5–3	2
1–2, or 2–1	2	3–6, or 6–3	2
1–3, or 3–1	2	4–5, or 5–4	2
1–4, or 4–1	2	4–6, or 6–4	2
1–5, or 5–1	2	5–6, or 6–5	2
1–6, or 6–1	2	Total Combinations	36

A given double, on the average, occurs only 1 time out of 36 possible rolls (odds are 35-to-1 against), whereas a non-double such as 2–1 occurs 2 times out of 36 possible rolls (odds 17-to-1 against). Non-doubles can occur in 2 different ways: 2–1, for example, can occur as 2 on the first die and 1 on the second, or 1 on the first die and 2 on the second. In actual games the two dice may be indistinguishable; this doesn't alter the fact, however, that non-doubles occur in 2 different ways.

Odds are calculated with the 36 possible dice rolls as the frame of reference. When we speak of 21 *ways* or 21 *combinations*, for example, we always mean 21 out of the possible 36 dice combinations, or 21/36.

In order to count the number of shots that hit a blot or blots, you don't have to learn elaborate tables of odds to cover different situations. With a little practice, anyone can learn to count quickly and accurately — no mathematical wizardry is required.

Counting shots is a much overrated skill. It is far more important to understand the underlying structure of the game than to be able to count shots rapidly. Even in positions where you don't want to be hit, there are almost always other considerations besides simply minimizing the number of shots you are exposed to.

Direct Shots

A **direct shot** is one in which a blot is 6 pips or less away from an opposing checker. There are several types of direct shots.

Single Shots

A blot exposed to one particular number is called a **single shot**.

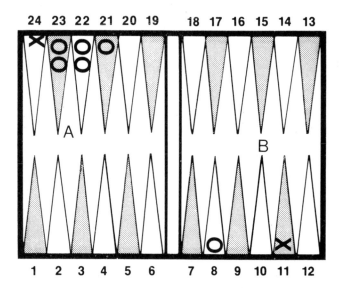

Position 1A–1B

In Positions 1A and 1B, O is exposed to a direct 3-shot. Let's compare the number of ways that X has to hit in both positions.

In Position 1A, X has a **simple direct shot,** that is, the blot may be hit by only a single specific number (a 3) showing up on either die.

By going through Table 1 and adding up all the combinations containing a specific 3 on either die, we find there are 11 combinations. *There are always 11 ways out of 36 to roll any one specific number.* This means that a simple direct shot will be hit just slightly less than 1/3 of the time ($^{11}/_{36}$).

In Position 1B, X has another single direct 3-shot. Here, however, X can hit not only with a *specific* 3, but also with combinations 2–1 and 1–1. This is not just a simple direct shot. To compute the total number of ways to hit, you begin by taking the base number 11 (the number of ways in which to hit a simple direct shot), and add on all the combinations that hit *without* a specific 3. In this case there are 3 extra ways to hit: 2–1 (2 ways) and 1–1 (1 way). This gives us a total of 14 ways.

Table 2 summarizes the chances of hitting a single direct shot (or of throwing a given number of 6 or less).

Table 2. Chances of Hitting a Single Direct Shot (or throwing a number 6 or less)

Number or Distance to Blot	Simple Direct Shot	Extra Possible Combinations	Total number of Ways to Hit	Probability of Hitting
1	11	0	11	$^{11}/_{36}$ or 31%
2	11	1	12	$^{12}/_{36}$ or 33%
3	11	3	14	$^{14}/_{36}$ or 39%
4	11	4	15	$^{15}/_{36}$ or 42%
5	11	4	15	$^{15}/_{36}$ or 42%
6	11	6	17	$^{17}/_{36}$ or 47%

When leaving a direct shot, the further away, the more likely to be hit. The 1-shot is hardest of all to hit since there are no extra possible combinations, while the 6-shot is easiest to hit, with 6 extra combinations. The chances of hitting a single direct shot vary from 11 ways (about ⅓ of the time) to 17 ways (almost even chance).

Double Shots

A **double shot** occurs when you have two direct numbers which hit (either two blots exposed to one opposing checker, or one blot exposed to two opposing checkers).

Position 2A–2B

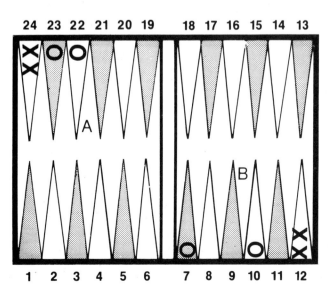

In Position 2A, X has a **simple double shot**, i.e., a shot with no extra combinations. He may only hit O with a specific 1 or a specific 2 which must appear on at least one die.

There are 20 ways out of a possible 36 rolls to hit a simple double shot. Intuitively, then, the basic double shot will be hit slightly more than ½ the time (if you add up all the possible combinations in Table 1 which contain a 2 or a 1, without counting any twice, you will obtain the same result: 20).

In Position 2B, X also has a double shot in his outer board: 2's and 5's. Here, however, X can hit not only with a specific 2 or specific 5, but also with combinations 1–1 and 4–1. This is not just a simple double shot. To compute the total number of ways to hit, you begin by taking the base number 20 (the number of ways in which to hit a simple double shot) and add on all the extra combinations that hit *without* a specific 2 or specific 5. In this case there are 3 extra ways to hit: 1–1 (1 way) and 4–1 (2 ways). 2–3 is not counted as an extra combination since it contains a specific 2 and thus has been already included in the basic 20 combinations. The total number of ways to hit is 23.

You may wish to practice your shot-counting by figuring the number of shots in the next slightly more complicated position.

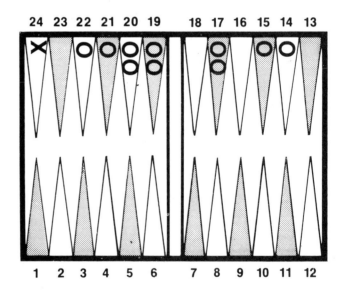

Position 3

If we analyze this position, we see that it is basically a double shot (2's and 3's), with some extra combinations. To compute the total number of ways to hit, you begin by taking the base number 20 (the number of ways to hit a simple double shot) and add on the extra combinations which hit and do not contain either a specific 2 or 3.

1–1 hits (1 way) and 6–4 also hits (2 ways) to give us a total of 20+1+2 or 23 ways to hit. 2–1, 6–3, and 3–3 are not counted because they are included in the total of simple double shots, and 5–4, and 5–5 are not counted because they are blocked. Note that the number of shots would be the same even if O did not have a blot on the fifteen point.

Triple Shots

A **simple triple shot** (when you have 3 specific numbers to hit, without combinations) occurs in 27 ways, or exactly ¾ of the time. When there are also extra combinations that hit, which do not include any of the 3 specific numbers, they must be added to 27 to give you a final total.

Other Multiple Direct Shots

A **quadruple shot** (with 4 specific numbers to hit) occurs in 32 ways, not counting extra combinations. With 5 different specific numbers to hit (a **quintuple shot**), there are 35 ways, and if all 6 numbers hit, there are, of course, 36 ways out of 36 possible rolls — in other words, any roll will hit.

Summary for Counting Direct Shots

If the shot is **direct** (6 pips away or less), whether single or multiple, begin with the base figure: $^{11}/_{36}$ (for a single shot), $^{20}/_{36}$ (double), or $^{27}/_{36}$ (triple). That base number will be the probability of hitting unless there are also additional combinations that hit. If so, add them to the base figure *without* including those which contain the specific number (or numbers) needed to hit. Also do not count combinations that are blocked.

Indirect Shots

An **indirect shot** is one in which a blot is 7 or more pips away from an opposing checker. Since there are no single numbers on one die which are 7 or more, you simply add up all the combinations on both dice which hit to compute the total number of shots.

To calculate the number of ways to hit a 9-shot, for example, you enumerate the possible combinations which add up to 9: 5–4 (2 ways), 6–3 (2 ways), and 3–3 (1 way) for a total of 5 ways. When you have a multiple indirect shot, you simply add up all the combinations of the number which hit, being careful not to count the same combination twice.

Table 3 shows the chances of hitting a single blot which is 7 or more pips away from an opposing checker. This table assumes that all possible combinations are playable; that is, that they are not blocked by opposing points. When certain combinations are blocked, you do not count them (or, if using Table 3, subtract them from the totals given). Note that the further away the indirect shot, the *less* likely it is to be hit (with the exception of a 12-shot).

Applications to Re-entering

When you are on the bar with a man against a 5-point board, you need 1 specific number to re-enter. Thus, the odds on re-entering are the same as hitting a simple (single) direct shot: $^{11}/_{36}$.

Table 3. Chances of Hitting a Single Indirect Shot
(or Throwing a Number 7 or more)

Number or Distance to Blot	All Possible Ways to Hit	Probability of Hitting
7	6	$6/36$ or 17%
8	6	$6/36$ or 17%
9	5	$5/36$ or 14%
10	3	$3/36$ or 9%
11	2	$2/36$ or 6%
12	3	$3/36$ or 9%
15	1	$1/36$ or 3%
16	1	$1/36$ or 3%
18	1	$1/36$ or 3%
20	1	$1/36$ or 3%
24	1	$1/36$ or 3%

Table 4. Probability of
Entering Opponent's Home Board
from the Bar

Number of Open Points in Opponent's Home Board	Number of Closed Points	Number of Ways to Enter	Percent of Successful Rolls
0	6	0	0%
1	5	$11/36$	31%
2	4	$20/36$	56%
3	3	$27/36$	75%
4	2	$32/36$	89%
5	1	$35/36$	97%
6	0	$36/36$	100%

Similarly, with 4 points closed and 2 points open, the odds of re-entering are $20/36$, the same as a double shot. This means that you stand to re-enter against a 4-point board slightly more than ½ of the time.

When 3 points are closed, you have the same chances of entering as hitting a triple shot: $27/36$. On the average, you will re-enter a 3-point board exactly ¾ of the time.

Many players are surprised by this last figure; they feel that they stay out of a 3-point board more than the indicated ¼ of the time. This feeling may be due to the psychological tendency to remember all the unlucky rolls you've gotten, while forgetting all the times that you easily came in against a 3-point board.

The chances of coming in against a 2- or 1-point board are $^{32}/_{36}$ and $^{35}/_{36}$ respectively. These odds correspond to the probability of hitting the rare quadruple and quintuple shots.

Summary

Once again we emphasize that it is not essential to memorize the exact totals and percentages in the tables of this chapter. If the basic concepts in this summary are fully grasped, you will be well equipped to deal with any situation where the odds are relevant.

The only numbers that need be remembered (and for which you should acquire an intuitive grasp) are the chances of hitting a simple single, double, or triple shot: $^{11}/_{36}$, $^{20}/_{36}$, $^{27}/_{36}$ respectively. These also represent the chances of re-entering with a single man against a 5-, 4-, or 3-point board. (Intuitively it may help to think of these probabilities as slightly less than $^1/_3$, slightly more than $^1/_2$, and exactly $^3/_4$.)

Any other probabilities of hitting may be derived from these three figures using the basic method of counting — that is, take the basic simple-direct-shot figure and then add to it extra combinations that hit. Indirect shots consist entirely of these extra combinations.

When leaving a single shot, you need not memorize Tables 2 and 3, or calculate the exact odds every time. The following basic observations will be sufficient to guide you to the correct play:

1. An indirect shot is much more unlikely to be hit than any direct shot. Indirect shots will occur frequently and are usually not the key consideration for a play. Because direct shots are much more likely to be hit, they should be avoided unless there is a good reason for leaving them.

2. When leaving a direct shot, the further away, the more likely to be hit. The 1-shot is hardest of all to hit since there are no extra combinations, while the 6-shot is easiest to hit with 6 extra combinations. The chances of hitting a single direct shot vary from 11 ways (about $^1/_3$ of the time) to 17 ways (almost even chance).

3. Unlike the direct shots, the further away the indirect shot, the *less* likely it is of being hit (with the exception of a 12-shot).

Glossary

Advanced Anchor: An anchor on the opponent's four or five point. See also **golden point**.

Anchor: A point held by player in his opponent's home board.

Automatic Doubles: If each player rolls the same number on the first roll of the game, the doubling cube remains in the middle but may be turned to 2. Players usually agree to limit the number of automatic doubles to one per game.

Backgame: A game where you hold two or more points in your opponent's inner board and you hope to hit him in the latter stages of the game as he attempts to bear his men in and off.

Backgammon: (1) A game of chance and skill played in a special board by two people; each has fifteen checkers which he moves according to the throw of the dice. (2) A **backgammon** or **triple game** occurs when the winner bears off all his checkers before his opponent bears off any, and does so while his opponent has one or more checkers in the winner's home board. In this event, the winner receives triple the points shown on the doubling cube. Outside the United States, a backgammon is only scored as a double game.

Back Man (back runner): A player's checker in his opponent's inner board.

Bar: The strip in the middle of the board which separates the inner and outer boards. When a checker is hit, it is placed **on the bar:** Checkers on the bar must re-enter the game in the opponent's home board. If a player has a checker on the bar, he cannot move any other checkers until all his checkers on the bar have been re-entered.

Bar Point: A player's seven point.

Bear (as in bear on a point, bear on opposing checker): A checker 6 or less pips away from a given point is said to bear on that point.

Bear In: To bring your checkers into your inner board in preparation for the bear-off.

Bear Off (take off): To remove a man from the board by playing him off your inner board according to the rolls of the dice.

Bear-Off: The final stage of the game where you remove your men from your inner board.

Block: To form points in front of your opponent, hindering his progress.

Blockade: A contiguous series of points established in front of your opponent to hinder his progress. See also **prime**.

Blot: An exposed or single checker on a point.

Board: (1) The entire backgammon table. (2) One of the four quadrants of the backgammon table, each quadrant containing six points. The quadrants are referred to as **player's home** or **inner board, player's outer board,**

opponent's home or **inner board** and **opponent's outer board** (see Chapter 1, Positions 1 and 2). (3) **1-, 2-, 3-, 4-, 5-, 6-point board:** The number of points closed in the inner board. A 6-point board is called a **closed board.**

Box (in the box, man in the box): The player in a chouette who plays alone against all the others.

Break the Board: To give up points you have established in your inner board.

Break a Point: To relinquish a point already owned.

Builder: A spare checker bearing on a point or blot.

Captain: In chouette play, the leader of the team playing against the man in the box. The captain moves the checkers and makes final decisions for his team.

Checker (counter, man): A playing piece, or man.

Chouette: A form of playing backgammon allowing more than two players to participate at one time. Rules are given in Chapter 1.

Close Out (shut out): To make all 6 points in your inner board while your opponent is on the bar.

Cocked Dice: Any die (dice) which lands illegally. Dice which have landed on a checker, off the board, or in any manner other than flush and flat on the half of the board on the player's right.

Combinations of the Dice: The number of possible rolls out of the possible 36 to accomplish a specific objective.

Come In or **come on, enter, re-enter:** To begin the course of the game again in the opposing home board after having been hit.

Consolation Flight: A secondary tournament for players eliminated from the main tournament.

Cover: (verb) To place a second checker on an exposed blot of the same color, thus making a point.

Cube (doubling cube, doubling block): A three-dimensional cube or block with the numbers 2, 4, 8, 16, 32, and 64 on it. It is used for raising the stakes and for indicating the amount of points being played. **Own, Control the Cube:** A player owns the cube after he has accepted a double from another player, until he re-doubles. The player who owns the cube alone has the right to re-double if he chooses. **Cube in the Middle:** Indicates the game has been doubled by neither player. Either player may offer the first double.

Cup (dice cup): Cup used to shake up and roll the dice.

Dice (singular: die): Small cubes marked with 1 to 6 spots on each face, used to determine the moves.

Double (give a little present to, turn the crank, twist): Increase the stakes of the game to twice their previous size.

Doubles (doublet): When both dice come up with the same number. Four units of that number are then taken by player.

Gammon (double game): When the winner of a game bears all his checkers off the board before his opponent bears off any, he wins a gammon, or twice the value on the cube.

Golden Point: The opponent's five point.

Hit (bump, knock off, send back): Move one or more of your men to a point occupied by a blot of your opponent.

Holding Game: A type of game where you hold a point or points in your opponent's inner or outer board in order to prevent him from safely coming home.

Home: Your inner board.

Jacoby Rule: Players can agree before the game begins that gammons and backgammons will count only as 1 point if the cube has *not* been doubled by a player during the course of the game.

Midpoint: A player's *thirteen* point (equals opponent's *twelve* point) where five men are initially stationed.

Pass: To refuse to accept the cube when doubled by the opponent, thus giving up the game and losing the value indicated on the cube before the double.

Pip: (1) The number of dots on the face of a die. (2) The units of movement; e.g., 3 pips forward means 3 units or points on the board forward.

Pip Count: A method of determining the relative standing in a race.

Prime: (1) 6 closed points in a row. (2) Also (loosely) any number of points in a row — e.g., a 4-point prime means four points in a row. **Break a Prime:** To open points in the prime. **Broken Prime:** A prime with a gap in it. **To Prime:** To form a prime. **Priming Game:** A type of game in which the chief objective is to trap some of the opponent's men behind a prime.

Quadrant: One of the four divisions of the backgammon table. Each quadrant contains six points.

Re-double: After accepting the cube and thus doubling the stakes of the game, a player can then re-double his opponent, again doubling the stakes.

Running Game (forward game): A type of game in which the chief objective is to enter as rapidly and efficiently as possible into a race.

Shot: An opportunity to hit a blot when the blot is in range of an opposing checker. **Direct Shot:** When a blot is 6 or less pips away from an opposing checker. **Combination or Indirect Shot:** When a blot is 7 or more pips away from an opposing checker — hence, a combination of both numbers on the dice is needed to hit it. **Single Direct Shot:** When only one number is available to hit directly. **Double Direct Shot:** When only two numbers are available to hit directly. **Triple Direct Shot:** When only three numbers are available to hit directly. **Number of Shots:** The number of rolls out of a possible 36 that hit (*not* the number of blots). **17-to-1 Shot:** A shot where the odds against hitting are 17 to 1, i.e., where there are two ways out of 36 of hitting. **35-to-1 Shot:** A shot where the odds against hitting are 35 to 1, i.e., where there is one way out of 36 of hitting.

Slot: To leave a checker exposed on a point you wish to make, hoping to cover it on the next roll.

Split: To separate two men which are together on a point.

Take (accept a double): To agree to receive the cube when doubled by the opponent and continue the game for double the previous stakes.

79-223

795.1
Ma

Magriel, Paul.
    An introduction to backgammon : a
step-by-step guide / Paul Magriel. New
York : Times Books, c1978.
    154 p. : ill. ; 26 cm.

1. Backgammon. I. Title